MEDITATION

for

NON

MEDITATORS

Learn to Meditate in Five Minutes

BY JANET NIMA TAYLOR

CONTENTS

Chapter 1

HIT THE PAUSE BUTTON

 Hit the pause button.

Wouldn't it be nice to have a remote control with a pause button that let you stop life for a few minutes, take a breath, and relax, knowing you could return to your regularly scheduled programming whenever you were ready?

That's what meditation is.

It's the simple, time-tested practice of creating a gap between stimulus and response, a pause between all the thoughts, emotions, sensations, and circumstances that arise every minute of our lives. Each moment, we have an opportunity to be aware of the sensation of our breath, stop for a moment or two, and determine a more skillful response. Most of us have already naturally experienced a few meditative moments in our lives.

Sometimes life might feel like a speeding train that we are running to keep up with. Other times, it might feel like a huge vat of mud has engulfed us—or maybe both at the same time.

Meditation can help clear away the years of dirt and debris of our past experiences to reveal our long-held beliefs, preconceived notions, biases, judgments, and opinions that may *or may not be* relevant to the present moment. Learning how to create this simple, yet powerful, gap gives us enormous freedom to explore new ways of responding to ourselves and to the world. We can slow down the runaway train, climb out of the mud, find a way to ease our suffering, and, yes, even find more happiness. Who wouldn't want some of that?

If you really just want to get to the part about how to meditate for five minutes, feel free to jump ahead to chapter seven. That's OK. I don't mind. When you are ready, you can come back to get some additional helpful information.

What is happiness? Note that there is a difference between pleasure and happiness. If you like chocolate cake and there is a cake in front of you, you could take a fork and bite into it, and you would most likely experience pleasure. Happiness, as we will use the word in this book, is a sense of well-being that is independent of any external situation or circumstance. We can cultivate a more consistent experience of happiness by systematically removing the obstacles we've created that keep us from feeling happy. We can break down these obstacles into the specific thoughts, emotions, sensations, judgments, conditioned reactions, and memories that caused us to think that external events and circumstances need to be just right for happiness to arise. Instead, imagine that happiness can be an inside job--it can be cultivated through a series of practices and a change in your perspective.

Here is a short history of my own learning about the difference between pleasure and happiness. In college, I was voted most likely to have a heart attack before the age of thirty. I had a frightening case of type A personality. I did everything full throttle: I graduated eighth in my class of 575 seniors in high school, finished my undergraduate degree in international relations in three and a half years—including six months of study in India—and then got an MBA. When I was twenty-eight, I raced into a corporate job that fed my anxiety and need for approval like methamphetamine. (For the record, I never tried meth, but I did watch *Breaking Bad*.)

I not only drank the corporate Kool-Aid of eighty-hour workweeks and nonstop thinking, I mixed it up by the bucket and handed it out to my staff to get them to produce more, better, faster. I was promoted and earned more every year, while marrying and divorcing husbands like I was trying on new shoes—they were fun until they hurt my feet, and I never had the patience to break a pair in. I just threw them away and tried another. If I sound callous and like a total bitch—yep, that was me. I spent at least a decade trying to figure out how to have the perfect life—husband, child, house, car, job. Externally, it all seemed to be working but, internally, I felt like a mess, as though if people only knew how screwed up I was, they would fire me immediately.

After many years of not enough sleep and too much work, I was worn down and unable to keep the ruse going. It stopped being worth the hassle. I dreaded going to work but couldn't figure a way out, and I was terrified to take a break—if I stopped racing, someone else would run past me in a second. Then where would I be?

I looked around for something that might ease my anxiety. Sex and alcohol worked well for a while but had awful side effects. I tried Prozac when it first came out—that made me feel like a zombie. I read books on mindfulness and meditation, something I began to explore during my college days in India, but now they weren't just mildly interesting topics. I felt like I was looking for something to save my life. I attended different meditation retreats. Some were too *woo woo* for me (crystals and pyramids and the like—not that there's anything wrong with those). Others were too rigid and strict ("You must sit exactly in this exact position or I will beat you"). I tried many methods, looking for something that I could easily do on a regular basis.

In 1998, I met an American meditation teacher named Lama Surya Das. He's a Jewish guy from Long Island, but he has studied and practiced Buddhism and meditation for over forty years and wrote a book entitled *Awakening the Buddha Within*. Suddenly, it all started to make sense. I went on a silent retreat in January, 1999 and knew I had found my meditation home.

This meditation does *not* have to be religious or spiritual in any way. It is a proven method of reducing the negative impact of stress, increasing happiness, and helping relieve other distraction-related problems such as eating disorders and depression. The meditation he teaches is alternately described as natural meditation or even non-meditation. It is *not* about trying to reach some exalted state or about trying to get your mind to stop thinking. It is about learning how to rest in the present moment without getting so entangled in the sensations, judgments, opinions, ideas, worries, stories, sounds, sights, fears, or whatever else arises within us or around us. **It is about learning how to give yourself a break, to give yourself permission to just sit, just breathe, and just be.**

The irony is that when I became a regular meditator, I not only found relief from my anxiety and Type *A* neurosis, but actually became a better, more effective manager. I went on to get a promotion in the midst of layoffs and downsizing. My employees were happier because I was more present with them and better supported them in being successful. Big companies are now discovering the benefits of mindfulness and meditation for their workers. Companies such as Google, Yahoo, Ford, Cisco, and HBO, find that making meditation easy and available is a great company benefit for healthier, happier, and more productive employees (for some examples, see *Wired Magazine,* June 2013).

As for me, I loved meditation so much that I eventually gave up the corporate life for a full-time job as a meditation teacher at a community center here in Kansas City, Missouri. (My children were grown and my partner passed away, so the timing in my life made it easier.) I have spent the last five years meditating every day with a wonderfully diverse group of people, many who never meditated before coming to the center. I have tested different kinds of meditation sessions and instructions and have gotten immediate feedback about what works and what doesn't, about what some people like and others don't. These daily sessions, my own experience, and my studies of the top experts in the field became the basis for this book.

Meditation does not have to be a chore, another item on the "to do" list of life. There can be joy and peace in the process, and there is value even in short meditations throughout the day. My teacher often says, "Many quickies are better than a few longies." We don't have to think in terms of quantity, but quality—how can I infuse a sense of meditative awareness into more moments of my life?

How do you feel about brushing your teeth? Is it something you do each morning and night? How would you feel about leaving home without brushing your teeth? Meditation can be the same as brushing your teeth. It can become a part of daily life that is so natural and easy that it would feel odd leaving home without having meditated, even for just five minutes. So instead of feeling the burden of adding an item to the never-ending "to do" list, how can we make it fun? This is the primary objective of this book: to make it fun, easy, and beneficial.

The words I've written are not the experience you are searching for. Words can merely point the way to having the direct experience. It's easy to confuse knowledge with wisdom. If it were possible to simply read a book about riding a bike and then fully know the experience, that would be great. However, we all know that reading a book about riding a bike might be nice, and it might make you a better biker in the long run, but it is no substitute for getting on a bike and attempting to stay upright as you peddle. Meditation is about changing behavior, not just about changing beliefs. We begin by imagining the possibility that there is a different way to experience ourselves and the world around us, then we have to try it out for ourselves.

To accomplish this transformation, it might be helpful to begin by addressing some of the most common misperceptions about meditation.

Chapter 2

WHAT MEDITATION IS *NOT*

Let's start with what many people think about meditation:

- I have to sit on the floor in the lotus position. (Nope.)

- I have to stop thinking. (Nope.)

- I'm Christian or Jewish or Muslim or atheist. Will meditating interfere with my faith? (Nope. Meditation can be completely nonreligious.)

- I have to sit still a long time. (Nope).

- I have kids; kids can't meditate. (They can and will—you'd be surprised!)

- I don't have time. (To breathe? Really?)

As little as five minutes of meditation each day can make a huge difference over time.

Where I work, we offer thirty-minute meditation sessions at 12:10 p.m. and 5:30 p.m. every day, 365 days per year. I have students and retirees, truck drivers and doctors, attorneys and the unemployed, young, old, happy, unhappy, the joyful, and the depressed. Every Tuesday, an attorney comes in, take his suit coat off, and lies on the carpeted floor with a cushion under his head. He tells me it makes him a better lawyer to chill for thirty minutes.

Let's discuss the details of these misperceptions and the truth about meditation:

- **"I have to sit on the floor in the full lotus position."** *Sitting in a chair works just as well.*

  I joke that you are equally likely to become enlightened sitting in a chair as you are wrapped up like a pretzel on the floor. My only suggestion is that you keep your back fairly straight and that your head rests comfortably upright on your shoulders. You might imagine a string gently pulling you up from the base of your spine, all the way through the crown of your head, letting the rest of your body relax. This position helps you remain more alert and less likely to doze off. You can place your hands comfortably on the tops of your thighs. It helps to place each foot on the floor. I encourage you to take your shoes off, but it's not necessary. You can even use this position while sitting at your desk at work—you don't even need to close your eyes. Your coworkers might think you just have great posture.

- **"I have to sit still for a long time."** *The amount of time is not important; giving yourself permission to do absolutely nothing for a few moments can have a very positive impact.*

  Research shows (see *The Relaxation Response* by Dr. Herbert Benson) that short amounts of time spent purposefully doing nothing can have significant impacts on your health and mental state. The more important factor is consistency—making the practice not only a daily habit, but one you practice throughout the day.

- **"I have to stop thinking."** *Nope, we're not trying to stop thoughts, but rather disentangle our attachment to them and identification with them.*

  Whenever I go to a party or function where I am asked, "What do you do?" I have heard a wide variety of responses over the past five years to my answer, "I teach meditation." Some people smile awkwardly (I think they might wonder if that is a "real" job), and then they change the subject ("Maybe she secretly stays home watching *Jerry Springer* and calls that *meditation*"). Some dismiss me with the swoosh of their hand. "Oh, I've tried to meditate, but I can't stop my thoughts." Boom. Done.

If they don't run away at that point, I have time to explain that meditation is *not* about trying to stop thinking. As we all know, the second you try to *not* think about a

pink elephant, there is a very big pink elephant in the middle of your brain.

When you practice meditation, you learn to disentangle yourself from identifying so closely with your thoughts. The thoughts (and emotions and sensations) might still arise, but you can begin to relate to them as if they are clouds in the sky—you neither try to hang on to them nor push them away. Find a balance between the two, where you are simply aware of whatever arises. When you no longer identify so strongly with your thoughts, they naturally slow down. It's like taking your foot off the gas pedal of a car--the car naturally starts to slow down.

Duke Tufty, my dear friend and cofounder of Serenity Pause, the name we have given our meditation program at the community center, often describes the image of being on the freeway at rush hour. The cars are all around you so it's difficult to change lanes. That is what our minds and thoughts are like most of the time. Now imagine that same freeway but at 3 a.m., when the nearest car/thought is perhaps a mile ahead or a mile behind.

We can practice creating a space between our thoughts so that we have time to respond more skillfully. There's more about this practice in the next chapter.

- **"Meditating will interfere with my religious beliefs."** *Meditation can be done in a completely nonreligious way.*

Webster's Unabridged Dictionary offers a secular as well as spiritual definition:

1: to engage in contemplation or reflection

2: to engage in mental exercise (as concentration on one's breathing or repetition of a mantra) for the purpose of reaching a heightened level of spiritual awareness

Having a spiritual belief has *nothing* to do with reaping the benefits of meditation. In fact, you don't even have to believe in meditation—just give it a try and see what happens. In my center, Christians come to meditate, along with Jews, Muslims, atheists, agnostics, and "spiritual but not religious" folks, as well as many who would not want to be identified by any label or limiting way.

I took this belief to Father Thomas Keating, who has been a Catholic monk for seventy years and who began meditating in the 1970s with Zen Buddhists. Father Thomas has been an iconic leader in the Catholic approach to meditation as a method for listening to God, rather than just talking to God. Father Thomas found that meditation practice benefitted him in many ways and, in fact, he created a meditation process using Christian words called "Centering Prayer." Decide for yourself. Give it a try. See what happens.

Jon Kabat-Zinn, a professor at University of Massachusetts Medical School, created a program entitled "Mindfulness-Based Stress Reduction" based on his own Buddhist meditation experience that is stripped of any religious or spiritual words or concepts, along with a stack of quantitative data that demonstrates the health benefits of meditation. Over a dozen books and medical research papers have been written about the qualitative and quan-titative findings on the benefits of meditation for mental and physical well-being as well as for stress and pain management. If you like diving into the details, check out Betty Wisner's study about the impact of meditation as a cognitive behavioral practice for alternative high school students: (http://repositories.lib.utexas.edu/handle/2152/18365).

I encourage you to suspend any previous ideas about what "meditation" is and what it is not. Simply try it with an open mind.

- **"I have kids—they can't meditate!"** *They can and will—even with you.*

I have kids, and I understand how exhausted and overwhelmed parents can become with all the scheduling and activities required to be a "good" parent. About three years ago, many parents phoned or e-mailed that they wanted to meditate but needed childcare to come to our center. We started providing babysitters, and then I met and became friends with a woman who taught meditation to children, including her own daughter, (now a beautiful, calm, and compassionate woman who is twenty-four years old). Peggy Mulvihill, with twenty-five years of elementary school and Montessori training, started our youth meditation program, and it became an instant success. I do not want to imply in *any way* that teaching every single child to meditate is a simple task. However, Peggy has come up with creative ways to help children concentrate on their breathing in order to learn self-regulation and practice visualizations to cultivate more positive mental states. It really works! You'll find videos of the kids at SerenityPause.com, and you can purchase Peggy's book, *Raising Calm Kids* at Amazon. com. (Thanks, Peggy!)

Peggy also creates opportunities for families to meditate together. Last February, we gave everyone a "love" challenge in honor of Valentine's Day. We handed out calendars and encouraged everyone to meditate for just five minutes a day and record their accomplishments and any reflections. We encouraged parents to engage their children in the month-long event and to meditate *together* with their children. At the end of the month, we were blown away by the positive impacts reported. Moms and dads told us that their kids reminded them at bedtime that they hadn't meditated yet that day and needed to do so before they went to sleep. It might have been to check off the box, or it might have been a ploy to stay up for five more minutes, but hey, whatever works. A coworker once had a sign in his office that read, "Children spell love T-I-M-E." Meditating together can be a creative way to give you and your children time to chill out and spend time together in a productive, fully engaged manner.

Kids love ringing bells to begin and end the meditation. It becomes a trigger for them to become aware of their breathing. Kids' meditation can be empowering, for them and for their parents. What better reason to learn meditation than to be a better parent and give your child this priceless gift of focus and calm?

- **"I don't have time."** *To breathe? Really?*

This is the number one reason people give me that meditation isn't for them. In our multitasking, schedule-filled "I have to be busy to be successful" culture, it might seem as though adding one more thing to the list is impossible. I encourage you to start with the simple task of being aware that you are breathing. (If you are not breathing, you do not need to meditate). The most successful meditators are the ones who start slowly, five minutes here and there, not the gung ho, macho, newbie meditators who try to sit for an hour in the morning and an hour at night, every day for the first week. I usually don't see them back the second week. Take your time. Consider this a lifelong pursuit. As my mama from Texas always said, "Little by little, a whole lot gets done."

Now that we have the misperceptions out of the way, let's dive into the three main methods of meditation.

Chapter 3

THE THREE METHODS OF MEDITATION

In this chapter, we'll cover three basic types of meditation practices: concentration, natural awareness, and positive imagery.

As noted meditation is simply learning to create a gap between stimulus and response. You can hit the pause button and rest in the present moment without getting so entangled in the sensations, judgments, opinions, ideas, worries, stories, sounds, sights, fears, or whatever else arises within us or around us. You have probably already had a few meditative moments in your life.

To better understand meditation, we'll divide the practice into three bite-size pieces: concentration, natural awareness, and positive imagery. Note that I haven't used the word *mindfulness*. Mindfulness has become a buzzword that has multiple meanings, so it helps to talk about meditation with greater specificity. Here are the three key components of meditation:

- **C** **Concentration:** This practice trains your mind to concentrate on one object (your thoughts, your sensations, a word, or an external item such as a candle). Strengthening your ability to focus produces positive effects mentally and physically and enables better decision-making. It can be as simple as focusing your awareness on the tiny sensations of breathing in and breathing out. Thoughts, feelings, and even sounds will continue to arise—include those in the process by imagining them to be clouds in the sky, floating in the background.

  Concentration practice lets you notice your thoughts, then disentangle your identification with them. You'll find that many thoughts arise throughout the day. There will be an exact moment when you realize you've been lost in a storyline, emotions, or some internal drama. Fantastic! I encourage you to celebrate the moments when you realize you are distracted. In those precise moments, you are fully present, if only for a split second. Then, simply return your attention, as many times as needed, to the sensation of breathing.

Something I found encouraging early in my meditation practice is that research shows that even if you think you are doing it wrong, just trying to meditate has a positive physical impact on you by reducing cortisol levels and blood pressure.

- **A** **Awareness:** This method retrains your experience of "you" and the world by going beyond any conceptual thought. In its various forms, it strengthens a natural awareness of being alive, simply aware of whatever is arising. Right now, how do you know that you are alive? What is this experience of "aliveness"? By practicing resting in this natural awareness, you begin to get beyond the usual "noise" of thoughts, emotions, sensations, and situations. In its more advanced state, the knower and the knowing are no longer separated.

Sensations, emotions, and thoughts still arise, but you can learn how to get disentangled from them. We practice being present and find a sense of peace and well-being that is not a result of any external situation, circumstance, idle thought, emotion, or sensation. We all have this innate sense of well-being within us—but it is usually covered up by our past experiences, our storylines, and the ways in which we seek to be happy in inherently dissatisfying ways. We can learn to go beyond the superficial and find a deeper peace that is within each and every one of us.

- **P** **Positive Imagery:** Research shows that practicing positive mental states, such as loving kindness and compassion, enables us to experience those states more often and more naturally in everyday life—like athletes who visualize their successful performances, including every sensation, every emotion, every thought. Guided meditation can be a helpful tool for this practice. (Check out the ones that can be downloaded at SerenityPause. com.) Conflicting thoughts will likely arise while you practice positive imagery. For example, while you practice cultivating a sense of loving kindness for yourself, you may have thoughts such as, "I'm not lovable," or, "I don't deserve to be loved." While you imagine what it would be like if you were lovable, you can lightly and ever so gently reflect on those conflicting thoughts. Ask yourself why you feel unlovable. See what else arises. Then return to imagining a loving and peaceful experience. In positive imagery, we gently balance imagining the positive mental state with reflecting on any conflicting thoughts or emotions that arise. This practice has been shown to re-wire your brain by increasing the neural networks devoted to positive mental states.

Make it a habit. It is important to have some quiet time dedicated to meditation, *and* these methods can be practiced in any moment of any day. Making meditation a habit accelerates the benefits, and we form habits by creating motivation for change. Remind yourself how much better you feel after you have meditated. Start with a chart to check the days when you have meditated to give yourself visual cues. You can practice awareness (and give yourself credit) while you eat, walk, interact with others, or do the dishes. Try single tasking! Be aware when you take a few breaths before responding and then choose more skillful words or actions—small successes can lead to bigger ones.

Congratulate yourself when you do better and forgive yourself when you screw up. Reduce the time between realizing that you screwed up and admitting it. Begin again and again and again. You will find that being more fully present in each moment slowly begins to arise naturally. That is an amazing experience and is the reason why people have practiced these techniques for thousands of years. There is plenty of history and research to validate this transformation, this ability we all have to rewire the brain to more easily rest in a state of well-being and calm.

Here are some practical ideas on how to integrate these methods into each moment of each day:

- **Phone calls:** Each time the phone rings, take one deep, aware breath before you answer and one more after you hang up. How wonderful to have a meditation reminder so close at hand! Be aware of how phone calls impact your thoughts, feelings, and sensations.

- **Red lights or standing in line:** Instead of letting irritation arise while you're driving or waiting in line, use that delay as an opportunity to breathe deeply and be aware of internal sensations, emotions, thoughts, and, externally, be aware of the people and circumstances around you. To culti-  vate a positive state of mind, try wish- ing everyone around you more happiness in their lives, simply by radiating out a sense of loving kind- ness and compassion for them.

- **A wristband:** Wearing a simple, plastic, colored bracelet can serve as a visual reminder to take a few deep, mindful breaths throughout the day. My teacher has a humorous one that says: "Meditate as fast as you can!"

- **Every time you walk through a doorway:** Take a moment to breathe and be fully present each time you walk through a doorway. Often, our minds are racing ahead to where we're going or continuing to process what happened in the room we just left. This simple practice helps create a precious little gap to regroup and re-focus throughout the day.

Even five minutes a day can have a significant impact on your health and well-being. Make a commitment to meditate for one month, and see what happens. There is even a free five-minute MP3 meditation at SerenityPause.com.

Chapter 4

HAVE A HIGHER PURPOSE

WHAT IS YOUR MOTIVATION?

This is where you begin. Why do *you* want to meditate? Why meditate at all? Who cares? When the going gets tough, you'll need to be clear about why you want to meditate. Meditation can be a powerful transformer, but it doesn't work if you just read or hear about it. It requires actual practice. It is helpful to be clear and precise about your motivation and intention. For example, when you want to lose weight, you remind yourself, "I want to wear that sexy dress to my high school reunion."

Why do you want to meditate? It's OK to begin with some less-than-esoteric motivation like, "I want to stop screaming at my boss and coworkers every day." Choose the encouragement that is exactly right for you.

Consider including a higher purpose for your meditation because practicing meditation impacts not only you but the people around you. Note that not everyone may be ecstatic with your newfound peaceful attitude. I know this to be true from personal experience.

My mother was in the hospital a month ago. At eighty-eight years old, she was dying, and the family had gathered to be with her as she took her last breaths. My dear family, like many others, has its share of dysfunction and disharmony, and, for many years, I was a major contributor. As I slowly integrated meditative awareness into my everyday life, I found my family to be less annoying and, of equal importance, they found me less annoying as well. However, on the occasion of my mother's passing, everyone's nerves were frayed and the tension was palpable. Being stuck in a small intensive care room for three days does not usually make for increased family harmony.

At one point, the nurse entered the room and picked up the phone and requested that a morphine drip be sent up from the pharmacy. When someone is dying, this is sometimes a signal that the end is nearing. Opportunities for one more lucid moment with your loved one may become increasingly less likely. Suddenly my niece shouted out to her, "We aren't ready for that!" That was true, but my assessment was that the nurse was just preparing for what would eventually be needed. In response to my niece's outburst, I fell into an old, reactive, unskillful pattern (that is an understatement but sounds so much nicer than what really happened). With a wave of my hand, I became, once again, domineering and dismissive. I spoke to my niece condescendingly. I don't remember my exact words, but it might have been something like, "Let it go! Calm down." She did not calm down (have you noticed how telling people to calm down often has the opposite effect?) She stormed out the room, vowing never to return and letting me know that I was still a bitch.

She was right. Her reaction forced me to realize that I had not responded in a skillful way, and, much to my surprise and my family's as well, I immediately admitted my error and apologized. I followed my niece into the hall and asked that she give me a chance to say how sorry I was. I told her exactly how I had acted unskillfully and that I wanted her to stay. She looked me directly in the eyes and said, "Janet, sometimes I hate your Buddhist bullshit." Then she hugged me, and we returned to the room to be with my mom. This may seem like a small altercation, but, in my family, this could have turned into a feud that lasted for years, with neither side willing to give an inch.

Meditative awareness enables you to be present with your thoughts, your words, and your actions. At first you might not catch yourself before you respond unskillfully, but you will slowly get quicker at saying you're sorry. That interaction changed the way I handled situations from that point forward, and my behavior helped changed the way my family got along in this most difficult of times.

My purpose for meditating is to be a more beneficial presence to myself, to my family, and to all beings. I am motivated to meditate because I am a nicer, more loving person when I do so, and I have found that life is more enjoyable when I am less of a bitch and more of a loving human being.

Having people call you on your bullshit can be enlightening—only you can ascertain if it is valid feedback or not. But listen carefully, and see what is yours to own. My niece, my daughter, and even my mother, who never meditated a day in her life until she was eight-seven years old, came to appreciate meditation simply because they experienced my being present in a different way than I had been before.

I encourage you to include in your motivation the impact you will have not only on yourself but also on others around you through your thoughts, words, and actions. The ripple effect can be tremendous. Don't underestimate the power of peace that begins within you.

What is your motivation for meditating? Stop right now and write down a motivating phrase or sentence that you can easily bring to mind when the going gets tough. Know it. Memorize it. Each time you begin a meditation, recall the greater good you are creating.

Then just do it.

Chapter 5

ARRIVING

How you start a meditation session is very important. It begins the moment you sit in the chair or on the cushion. This might seem like a simple process, but you are encouraged take your seat with great awareness, to fully arrive, and consciously make the decision to devote the next few minutes to sit with inspiration and dedication. The minimal instructions on posture are: have a fairly straight spine with your head resting upright on your shoulders, and the rest of your body relaxed. Open up your lungs so you can breathe freely. So often these days, we scrunch down in front of a computer screen, solely focused on the screen and in our heads. Meditation is about getting our full body involved. **We sit like a mountain, strong and upright.**

Next, choose whether to meditate with your eyes opened or closed. I encourage you to consider opening your eyes, even for a bit, in order to more fully expand your awareness. There may be distractive movements in and around you, but they are like the distracting sounds you hear: let them become like clouds in the sky. We see and we hear them, but we do not focus on those distractions. We continue to return our attention to the sensation of breathing. **We imagine our breath like the wind in order to more fully connect ourselves with the world around us.** Meditation is not only about experiencing our internal sensations and thoughts more fully, but also about feeling more interconnected and interdependent outwardly with the world around us.

At first, all this straight sitting and eye gazing might feel a little uncomfortable and contrived. Do you remember how it felt when you first drove a car? I vividly recall my Driver's Education class in high school. The first time I got behind the wheel, I drove down a street and sideswiped a few parked cars, while the instructor screamed at me to pull over—he was a little shaken up! How odd and difficult it felt to put all the driving piece parts together. After more practice, and a few tickets (and an accident…or two), I became more comfortable and at ease in my car. This is the experience that occurs over time with your meditation practice: arriving fully, finding the best way for you to sit, and then doing it over and over again until it feels natural and easy. When you realize you are slouching, that is a moment of awareness. Oh happy day! Hurray! You can then sit up straight again and again. This practice also does wonders for your posture.

You might add a sense of royalty to sitting down, as though you are a queen or king upon a throne. Inject the power of this action with an intention to be of service to all beings. Hold your head up straight, keep your shoulders back a bit, and prepare your body and mind for reigning over your experience.

Another very important factor is to integrate the experience of our body and our mind. In western culture, we spend a lot of time in our head. There are many ways in which we can just live in our head and think about our body as simply a vehicle that transport our brain around. Meditation is the practice of balancing awareness of the body and the mind together. We use the breath as our balancing point, experiencing the breath like the wind—fully integrated with your surroundings. We are conscious of breathing in and breathing out, and we are aware of the mind and the body at the same time: the sensations, the emotions, the thoughts and the sights. We practice finding a balanced awareness of both. Stop for a moment right now and just breathe with this sense of balancing body and mind, the inner experience with the outer stimuli. This simple practice can, over time, become your natural way of experiencing yourself and the world. Little by little, we awaken.

It is also helpful to imagine the **mind being like the sky**—vast and spacious. So often, our minds feel crammed full and constrained. When we open our mind to the vastness of space, there is a sense of greater knowing, of having access to the innate wisdom that is found not only within us, but also all around us. Instead of focusing solely on our limited experiences, imagine that you can access the wisdom of the ages—of, in fact, the universe. We open ourselves up to this greater experience of being alive.

At the end of each meditation session, instead of immediately jumping up and going back to being distracted, it helps to close with some clarity and distinction. It can be the ringing of a bell or a moment of gratitude. Even if the world seems to be crumbling around you, even if the meditation session felt awful, you can stop and reflect on how blessed you are in some way, even for the fact that you are still breathing at the end of the session.

Another ending is to take whatever benefit you feel you received from the meditation and imagine sharing it with all beings. Recognize and reflect upon—as so many meditation practitioners have for done for thousands of years—that we meditate not only for ourselves, but for the entire world. I am convinced that each person who spends time in meditation not only transforms themselves, but also transforms the energy of the world, if even just a bit.

These tiny steps--starting with arriving, then settling in with inspiration and dedication, and ending with clarity—this is what turbo charges meditation. Join me in this simple commitment to sit for yourself and for the world, and know that you are making a difference by doing it.

Chapter 6

HOW TO MEDITATE

Finally! Here are the detailed steps of how to meditate...

This meditation includes the three types of meditation described. (There are more details on each of the three meditation types in later chapters.) Practicing meditation out in the "real" world can sometimes be a challenge. It helps to create a special time and space to practice with fewer distractions and difficulties, both at home by yourself and out in the community with others.

CREATE A SPECIAL SPOT IN YOUR HOME TO MEDITATE. This spot can simply be a chair in the corner or a mat and cushion on the floor in front of a table of inspiring objects or pictures. My home meditation spot is simply a converted bedside table. I can fall out of bed each morning onto my meditation cushion. The reason to have a regular spot is that it creates visual cues which encourage you to meditate.

When I lived in a tiny apartment in Dallas, I didn't even have room for the mat and cushion to be out all the time (or so I told myself). I stored them under the bed and had to pull them out in order to meditate. I found that extra step of pulling out the mat and cushion reduced the likelihood of me meditating by about 50 percent. Just as setting your gym clothes out the night before helps you get to the gym, having a ready meditation spot in your home increases the chances of you actually doing it. Morning is usually best so that nothing gets in the way of a short meditation, but evening can work as well. Or do both!

NOTE: There is no special equipment needed, just your breath and your intention, although it is fun to pick out a pretty mat and cushion...and sometimes making a financial investment in a good mat and cushion or some fancy pillow or chair may increase your motivation to meditate.

THE KEY STEPS OF MEDITATION

HELPFUL TIP: You can either record yourself reading these instructions, or you can download a free MP3 recording from SerenityPause. com.

1. **Find a fairly quiet place.** There may still be dogs barking and horns honking, but reduce the external stimuli as much as possible. *My strong recommendation*: create a technology-free zone—*turn off the phone*. I discourage you from using your cell phone as a timer. I'm not a fan of the mobile apps that give you meditation timers. For many of us, our phones are too seductive. Glancing at the phone to see what time it is becomes checking to see if there's a message, which can lead to total distraction. A simple digital kitchen timer will do a fine job of timing your meditations. Find one that doesn't make any noise except for the final beep, and even better if it fits in your pocket. You can buy one at many different stores or use a link at SerenityPause.com. Most are less than ten dollars. Technology and social media are wonderful to support your meditation practice. However, sometimes it is best to keep things simple.

2. **Use this beginner's tip.** When you are new to meditation, you might find it helpful to place a pen and a small notebook next to you, open to a blank page. There may be a particularly difficult thought or worry that you can't seem to "see as a cloud in the sky" while you are meditating. Try writing it down and giving yourself permission to set it aside until after the meditation. You can always pick it back up when you are done. The worry will be there on the page waiting for you to return.

There is something powerful about writing your problem down and physically setting it aside. Research shows that people make better decisions when they set a problem or issue aside for a few minutes and do something completely different before returning to it.

As you become more experienced with meditation, it will become easier to allow thoughts and worries to come and go, but in the meantime, the notebook and pen can be a simple tool to improve your meditation experience.

3. **Decide upfront how long to sit.** You can choose five minutes or thirty minutes—but be specific. I encourage new meditators to start with just five minutes each day, then slowly increase the amount of time they sit. Set the timer so you don't constantly wonder if the time is up. *The timer is a critical component* of a successful meditation. Otherwise, it often happens that, in about three minutes, you suddenly need a drink of water or decide to go wash your hair or need to be sure you turned the stove off or dozens of other thoughts that might pop into your head.

4. **Decide on your sitting position.** You do not *need* to sit in any special position. It *helps* to sit with your back fairly straight and your head resting comfortably, balanced on your shoulders. Sitting on a mat and cushion on the floor

can feel comfortable over time. Some people prefer to sit in a chair (with feet flat on the floor). Some people have health challenges or physical ailments that require them to lie on the floor or in bed. Whatever position *you* are most likely to meditate, that is the best position for you.

If you sit on a mat and cushion on the floor, you can cross your legs in front of you or sit on your knees with legs stretched out toward the side. To keep your back fairly straight and your head upright, imagine pulling gently on an imaginary string from the base of your spine all the way up through the crown of your head. Place your arms in a comfortable position on the top of your thighs. The rest of your body can be relaxed.

Find a gentle position in which you can sit still without too much discomfort. An itch or pain of some kind may arise. Before immediately scratching or moving, try to just be aware of the sensation. You can scratch or move a little if it gets too overwhelming.

5. **Consider meditating with your eyes open.** Meditation can be done with your eyes opened or closed, but I recommend that you try meditating with your eyes open at least part of the time. This helps you incorporate the entire moment-by-moment experience into the meditation, and makes it easier to take the practice into

everyday life. If you're sleepy, it helps keep you from falling asleep. In fact, there is an ancient practice of rolling the eyeballs around in one direction and then the other whenever the feeling of sleepiness arises. Visualizations and positive imagery are usually done with eyes closed.

6. **Take a few slow, deep breaths.** Breathe in counting to four, and breathe out counting to six a few times to allow the body to settle in and settle down.

7. **Focus your awareness.** Bring awareness into the room and into your body. Become aware of the sensation of how your feet feel against the floor.

8. **Set your intention.** For the next few minutes, give yourself permission to set aside any need to reflect on the past or think about the future. Give yourself this precious gift of simply being present—the gift of just sitting, just breathing, and just being. Oh happy day!

9. **(Optional) Ring a bell three times.** While this isn't necessary, it can create a Pavlovian response that causes your body to relax when you hear the bell at the beginning and end of each formal meditation session.

10. **Get your voice involved.** It can be very helpful to include some Breath Yoga at the beginning of each meditation. Many people find that the sound and vibration of

their voices deepens the sense of being present. This practice is seen in the chanting and singing that often accompanies a meditation process. Research now measures the slowing of the heart rate when a slow, rhythmic sound is sung. Breath Yoga can be as simple as taking a deep breath in and then saying the syllable, "Ah" as you breathe out completely. The important aspect is to breathe in and out fully. I usually do it seven times, but feel free to do it three times or thirty, whatever feels right to you.

11. **Allow the breath to find its natural rhythm.** Most people are often unaware of how (or even if!) they are breathing. Most of the time, our breathing is shallow and tentative. Take this opportunity to explore what natural breathing feels like: not overly deep and full, and not too shallow and weak. Find your comfort zone for breathing in and breathing out.

12. **Gently focus attention on the experience of breathing.** Be directly aware of all the tiny sensations of breathing in and breathing out. Imagine that you experience each breath as if you were breathing for the first time—how amazing might that feel? Gently concentrate on your breath as the focal point for your attention.

13. **Imagine any thought, emotion or sensation as just a cloud in the sky.** We can be aware of them, but not focused on

them. Most of us spend a lot of time either rehashing the past or fantasizing about the future. Either can be pleasant or painful, but both take us away from being fully present in the moment. **Meditation is *not* a practice of trying to push thoughts, emotions or sensations away, but rather a practice of simply being aware of them,** like clouds in the sky, without getting so entangled with them and the stories we often create about them.

We can accept that it is the nature of the mind and the body to think and feel and hear and smell. In meditation, you don't try to stop these things from occurring but instead change the way you interact with them. Rather than getting distracted by a thought or emotion or judgment or opinion or story or sensation, imagine each one to be just a cloud in the sky. Practice finding the balance between trying to hang on to a particular thought or feeling, and *not* trying to push anything away, seeing them all as clouds in the sky.

You can begin to make friends with your thoughts, emotions and sensations in three ways: by not pushing them away, not clinging to them, and not ignoring them. **Practice being aware of them in the background while continuing to focus attention on the sensation of breathing.**

14. **Refocus after moments of distraction.** It happens to everyone. One moment we're concentrating on our breath,

and the next thing we're distracted by some idea or itch or whatever else arises. It may last a minute or for the entire meditation session. There will be an exact moment when you realize that you're distracted (either through awareness or it might be when the timer goes off). *It is important to celebrate each of those moments!* Those are moments of pure awareness. You woke up for a moment. Yahoo! Then simply refocus your attention, again and again, as many times as needed, on the sensation of breathing in and breathing out.

15. **Release into awareness.** After a few minutes of focusing on your breath, release your attention on your breath and allow simple awareness to naturally arise. Release the need to focus on anything specific; just be aware of being alive, aware of whatever arises internally as a thought, feeling or sensation, or whatever arises externally around you. Imagine the possibility of simply sitting for a few minutes with nothing to do or undo, nothing to fix, nothing to change, just resting in spacious natural awareness. Leave everything just as it is, and rest your weary mind. Thoughts, emotions, and sensations may still arise, but you no longer need to engage with them in any way. You'll learn to allow things to arise and fall away in their own time.

If you start to feel a bit fuzzy or distracted, you can always return to concentrating on your breath.

16. **Practice positive imagery.** When you have time, include a guided meditation with positive imagery. There are examples in the following chapters. Or you might simply spend a few minutes wishing for your own and other's happiness: "May I be happy." "May you be happy." While you silently say these words, imagine in great detail what it would feel like to have a deep sense of happiness and well-being that is unrelated to any external circumstances. Practice cultivating a positive mental state of happiness and well-being.

17. **Close.** It's helpful to have a common closing for your formal meditation process, as we discussed in the previous chapter. You can end with a sense of gratitude for having the time to meditate, and, if you like the bell, you can ring it three times at the end. You did it. Hurray.

ADDITIONAL MEDITATION PRACTICES:

- **Walking meditation:** When you have trouble sitting still, or simply for some variety, you can practice walking meditation in several different ways. First, there is a deliberate, slow walk, either inside or outside. If you go outside, be prepared for some weird looks. Our meditation center is in an urban area. At a recent daylong retreat, a young man in our group decided to go to the very top of a three-story parking garage and slowly, meditatively walk from one side to the other. Unfortunately, people in the surrounding buildings who were looking down at him, were apparently wondering "Why is this guy walking slow?" So, they called the police. There is no law against walking meditation, but be prepared to ignore weird looks or perhaps find a park or more conducive area for this practice. Slow walking is a strange sight in our culture!

Another walking practice is to break down the experience of walking into smaller components. "I'm raising my leg; I'm moving my foot forward; I'm placing my foot on the ground." Bring awareness to the tiny sensations of walking. This practice is usually done in a straight line back and forth over a specific area inside or outside.

The final walking practice is simply walking without doing anything else, including turning off the cell phone. Take a walk in the woods, or down the street, or to the park, and bring awareness to the entire experience. You might even swing on a swing or try skipping along, using your meditation skill of natural awareness. Bring a sense of lightheartedness to your walking meditation—try smiling as you walk!

- **Lying down meditation:** This option can help you when you have trouble falling asleep or wake up in the middle of the night. It also helps to bring awareness to the first moments when you awake each morning. Before you get out of bed, become aware of your breath, and set your intention of being aware of your breath as much as possible throughout the upcoming day.

- **Sky gazing:** This is an actual meditation practice and is one of my favorites. Find a comfortable outdoor chair or simply lie in the grass or on the sand at the beach. Begin with the preliminaries of meditation, as described above. Then just release. Let go of even the sense that you are meditating. Stare up at the sky with a gentle gaze, not focused on anything in particular, just aware of awareness. Don't try to meditate, just be fully present and aware, moment-by-moment.  Allow thoughts and feelings and sensations to simply come and go. No place to go, nothing to do, resting in the natural perfection of just living. See the innate perfection in things left just as they are.

Jack Kornfield, a well-known meditation instructor and author, says that 50 percent of meditation is simply self-acceptance: accepting ourselves, others, and everything the way they are in this moment. Carl Rogers, a noted psychologist, says we must first accept ourselves before we can truly change. Sky gazing in specific, and meditation in general, can be a practice in acceptance.

- **Meditate with others:** Having a support system of other people can turbo-charge your meditation practice. I'll talk more about this in a future chapter.

Here are some additional tips for integrating meditation, awareness and positive imagery into everyday life. With so much hubbub in life, our minds have been trained to stay constantly busy. You can start meditating by finding the missing moments in your life. We all have them—like when you're standing in line at the grocery store, or you might be early for a doctor's appointment. Imagine that instead of being irritated when you have to wait, you think, "Yippee! I now have some time to meditate."

- It might be as simple as taking three deep breaths, or just focusing on your breathing for a few moments. You can use your headset without turning any music on to signal that you are in your own space. Or you can listen to a guided meditation while you are commuting to work.

- Consider creating a few minutes each day when you are in a technology-free zone, sitting in the park or in the cafeteria, just observing everything and everyone around you.

- Use the stall in the bathroom as your secret hideout—a great place to meditate while at work.

- Sit at your desk with your computer monitor turned off, your phone on Do Not Disturb, and your cell phone on vibrate, eyes opened or closed, and give yourself a few minutes of doing nothing.

- Spend five minutes meditating before you start your car or right after you turn it off.

- Enlist your friends into eating in silence for ten minutes (more on eating meditation in chapter ten).

Over time, these moments become minutes, and minutes lead to a daily practice, and before you know it, life feels a lot less hectic and lot more fun.

ONE LAST THOUGHT ON MEDITATION:

DON'T WORRY ABOUT DOING IT "WRONG"

People often think they're not meditating correctly. Many people think that everyone else is getting it right *except* for them. I have certainly had this experience as well.

Early in my meditation practice, I read a book by Herbert Benson entitled *The Relaxation Response*. He studied people before, during, and after a fifteen-minute meditation exercise. He measured cortisol levels and blood pressure and interviewed them about their experiences. What he found was that while the subjects often didn't think they meditated correctly, but their attempts were enough to lower their stress levels. Just trying to meditate had positive impacts on their physical conditions. This research gives me great hope. Even when I sit down to meditate and feel like it isn't going well, something is shifting within me. I am slowly rewiring my brain. There is no litmus test for a single meditation session—merely that you showed up, you sat down, and you tried. That is enough for transformation.

There are times when meditation will feel so awesome that you feel blissed out, and there will be other times when meditation feels like the most painful thing you can imagine doing. A word of encouragement: it gets easier over time.

Meditation works on the body and the brain in subtle ways. Over time, it works its magic and enables you to live a more peaceful and joyful life. *Yes!* It is possible for you to be happy regardless of your external circumstances, mercurial hormones, random thoughts, and unpredictable emotions.

Chapter 7

THE FIVE-MINUTE MEDITATION

Getting started with any new behavior is difficult. Let's make this as easy as possible. Could you meditate for five minutes for the next thirty days? That would be enough to begin rewiring your brain for greater peace and calm in your life. Here's a simple five-minute meditation. I have created the acronym, P.E.A.C.E. as an easy reminder. Here's how it goes:

1. **Prepare:** Find a quiet area with a comfortable chair and give yourself permission to do absolutely nothing for five minutes. Create a technology-free zone and set a timer for five minutes.

2. **Exhale:** Take a few slow, deep breaths, inhaling to a count of four and exhaling to a count of six.

3. **Allow:** Allow your breath to find its natural rhythm, and be aware of breathing calmly.

4. **Concentrate:** Focus on the sensation of breathing. If thoughts or feelings arise, imagine them to be like clouds in the sky. Practice finding the balance between pushing thoughts, emotions, and sensations away and hanging on to them. When you realize you are distracted, simply return to concentrating on breathing.

5. **Ease:** After a few minutes, let go of your focus as you allow yourself to simply sit in your natural state—nothing to do or undo, nothing to fix or change, just sitting in awareness and ease.

This five-minute meditation is a great place to start. There's even a free five-minute meditation MP3 at https://serenitypause.com/free-5-minute-meditation/. Enjoy, and let me know what you think. You can e-mail me at janet@serenitypause.com.

Chapter 8

CONCENTRATION

Meditation often begins with the concentration practice. I describe it as finding a point of focus like the breath or a word such as "peace" or "calm." This technique is a powerful process that can be used throughout the day to bring your mind back to the present moment. The mind often flits from thought to thought, and we can gently pull it back to the point of focus. Understand that the concentration is not hard-edged and intense, like those staring contests we used to have as kids (or maybe you still have them?). This concentration practice is more gentle and delicate. Some describe it as placing about 40 percent of your attention on the point of concentration. With a gentle focus, we are still aware of thoughts, emotions, sounds, and sensations—like clouds in the sky—that arise within and around us.

What about this word *mindfulness*?

There is some confusion about the word *mindfulness* as it is used in the practice of meditation. In some meditation traditions, it is used in the way that concentration is described above: being mindful of our breath. In other traditions, the word *mindfulness* is more like the natural awareness that is described in the next chapter. Sometimes it's a combination of the two. In order to clarify exactly what activity is taking place, I prefer to use concentration and awareness as two separate words and definitions. **These two techniques can be used in conjunction with each other—as we meditate, we can decide to release the concentration point and release fully into natural awareness. When our natural awareness gets fuzzy, we can refocus our attention on the breath for a few moments to bring us back to being more present, and then return to natural awareness.**

The ability to concentrate is a powerful tool for whatever task we need to get done. In traditional texts, concentration is further defined using the three subcategories of familiarity, remembering to remember, and non-distraction. These nuances help us further develop our concentration abilities.

First, there are a myriad of ways to become more familiar with the experience of concentration. When we begin with focusing attention on the breath, we soon get distracted and return to the sensation of breathing, again and again. We gain much greater familiarity with what it feels like to pay attention and to concentrate on the breath by incorporating the practice into as many moments as possible during the day. Right now, as you read this book, you can also be aware of your breath in the background. In fact, as you meditate consistently, you'll become more aware of your breath throughout the day. You become more familiar with the feeling. In meditation, we concentrate *gently* on the breath to become familiar with it so that it happens more naturally more often.

Second, we remember to remember. Remembering our breath becomes part of our objectives throughout the day. I was at the meditation center one Saturday when a beautiful young woman was getting married there (in another room). I left the small meditation room as she and her father waited in the hallway outside for their cue to walk down the aisle of the main sanctuary. This was a big wedding—a dozen bridesmaids and groomsmen. There had clearly been months of planning, and everyone and everything looked magnificent. I saw the bride's face and what was her expression? Terror. Her brow was scrunched and worried, her eyes a little spaced out, as though she was trying to remember a thousand details in one moment. I smiled and said the usual, "Don't forget to breathe!"

She look directly at me, a bit surprised, took a giant gulp of air—and laughed. She said, "Thanks! I forgot to do that!" I could see in her demeanor that her mind was racing, wondering, worrying, planning, judging, hoping—whatever brides usually think about seconds before they get married. In the most important moments in our lives, but also in the more mundane ones, we can practice remembering to remember to breathe. It seems so cheesy, but physiologically, it works wonders on our bodies. We are so often oxygen-starved because of the wimpy, weak breaths that have become a habit.

The third distinction is non-distraction. We must be careful not to beat ourselves up too badly on this one. Distraction is the playground of the mind—we love to be distracted. It often feels so good, and sometimes it's even necessary. So before I extol the virtues of non-distraction, I'll give a shout-out to the value of distraction and the fact that it can be beneficial. For example, if you diligently work on a problem and feel stuck, it helps to do something completely different for a while. Sometimes when you find it too difficult to sit with meditation, it's best to get up and take a walk.

There is scientific research on this phenomenon. People who are put together to solve a complicated problem will do better if they take a break to do something different that distracts them from the problem, as compared to another group of people required to stay at the task without any break. As a new meditator, after first doing your best to stay with a meditation session, if the pain, a thought, a sensation, or some worry simply will not subside, it's OK to distract yourself for a bit.

Be careful, however, as the mind loves this little loophole. The mind might think, "Yay! It's OK to be distracted." Allowing distraction is unleashing the mind to run around for a bit, but don't get sucked into a mental black hole and forget to rein it back in after a while.

Distraction comes in two varieties: skillful and unskillful. Skillful distractions are healthy and not harmful to ourselves or others. Unskillful distractions are harmful to ourselves and/or others. Skillful distractions could be as simple as watching a movie or going for a walk. Unskillful distractions come in many varieties and forms: for example, you may feel a need for distraction due to some stress or struggle, so you go to a bar, have multiple cocktails, and pick someone up to have sex with—which all may seem like a really good idea at the time and may take your mind off any troubles, but in some cases causes more suffering in the long run.

Distraction can be seductive and can engage the mind fully in a myriad of ways that are not always beneficial. In the end, the most skillful place to return is to concentrating on the breath. We benefit from returning from the storyline; from the bunny trail; from the off-road mind excursion to get back to the here, to the now, to the breath.

Our culture has designed many wonderful tools for distraction. In an attempt to be more intentional with TV watching, I ordered Netflix, a program that allows me to choose specific programs to watch when I want to watch them. What a great idea. Then I discovered that Netflix has more options for distraction than I ever imagined possible!

We can cultivate the skill of non-distraction through the practice of concentration. It enables us to understand exactly what is going on in our minds and our bodies, moment by moment. In meditation, we return to the breath again and again, simply and, most importantly, gently.

Many of us have drill sergeants in our brains that judge us harshly for having become distracted in the first place. "You idiot," the voice might say. "You are never going to get this. Everyone else is probably doing it right except you." The mind can be a mean master that wants to wear you down so it can return to its incessant thinking.

The irony is that thinking sometimes feels like a security blanket that makes us feel safe, but ultimately it *cannot* bring us a sense of long-lasting well-being. The mind wants to assess our options, analyze every situation, and try to guess what others might be thinking. The mind can be a faithful servant but a poor master. We practice non-distraction because only then do we realize that we can control our responses to whatever thoughts, emotions, sensations, or situations might arise.

Concentration is a powerful tool to transform our experiences of living. It is the first, most important, step of the meditation process. Next up is awareness, the best friend of concentration and another powerful ally in our journey to finding and experiencing more peace and calm.

Chapter 9

AWARENESS

Another top technique for meditating is cultivating awareness. As described earlier, this method is about learning to rest in the most natural state—not trying to concentrate on an object, not trying to do or undo anything, but rather practice just being. This may sound silly—"aren't we just being all the time?" However, most people spend much of their time almost completely unaware of whatever is arising in the present moment.

I was surprised to learn recently that, as a nation, we now spend more time watching TV shows about cooking than we spend actually cooking—hmmm. You might examine how much time you spend involved in activities that require no awareness of the present moment. Have you ever sat down at the computer to check an e-mail and found yourself still there, hours later, watching cute cat videos? (Or is that just me?)

We can learn to be more intentional in the way we allocate our time. Keeping a journal of how you spend your time lets you to become more intentional in how we use this precious gift. Making time and taking time for meditation is a key factor in receiving the benefits of this amazing practice.

Once you have re-collected some of the time lost in distraction, you will have more time to practice meditation. We begin with concentration and then release into natural awareness, a powerful process for our time in an actual meditation session, as well as in all those moments when we want to be more fully present. We can sit in silent meditation, walk down the street, sit on a park bench, or gaze up at the sky, all with a sense of awareness and amazement of this precious experience of living.

Cultivating awareness helps us develop a playful curiosity about what exactly is happening in each moment. Each moment becomes an experiment in observation. It can also be practiced as we interact with another person—we give that person our full, undivided attention, without checking our phones or multitasking in some other way. Natural awareness is sometimes call non-meditation because we are not trying to *do* something. Sensations, emotions, and thoughts still arise, but through this delicate practice of awareness, we no longer get so entangled in them.

The other day, I was teaching a class on natural awareness, and we heard the sounds of children playing on the playground near the room where we were meditating. I encouraged everyone to bring the experience of hearing the children playing into their awareness as part of the meditation. The laughter and shouting reminded me how valuable being playful can be.

After we completed the meditation, I asked everyone to share their experiences. One courageous person spoke up and said that listening to the sounds of children playing brought up an intensely painful memory of being repeatedly scolded by the nuns when she went to Catholic school. This strong memory of an experience held over many decades still caused a sense of unworthiness, and that intense feeling arose simply from being aware of the sound of children playing. By realizing this connection to a deep hurt, she was able to shine upon it the light of awareness and begin to undo this misconception.

This is the power of awareness. We simply allow ourselves to be aware of whatever arises moment by moment. We allow our memories and emotions, sensations and thoughts to arise and be "seen" as clearly as we can.

We often hear that meditation is about "letting go," but that is only half the practice. My meditation teacher points out that trying to let something go is more about pushing away than about processing. He would say, "Let things come and go." We allow it all to arise, be experienced, perhaps examined, *then* allow it to go.

As you sit in natural awareness, you might become aware of what is happening internally as well as externally, and how the two go hand-in-hand. Practicing natural awareness can help us utilize the old emotions and thoughts that arise as tools for our awakening going forward. The moments when we realize that we feel stuck or are having unskillful thoughts or feelings are moments of awareness. We can use that as moments of praise: "Yahoo! Fantastic! I now see where I'm stuck."

Seeing that you're hooked is the vital first step. Slowly, the stranglehold those thoughts and emotions have over our reactions begins to loosen.

When you experience a realization, journaling can be an excellent tool for remembering and fleshing out the 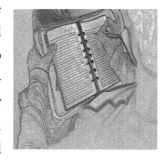 details of what exactly got you stuck, and what you can do differently next time to choose a better response. Articulating whatever thoughts or emotions arise, either through journaling or through talking to a trusted friend, can help us process and reframe our perspective.

We all wake up each morning (the fact that we wake up and are still living should, in and of itself, be celebrated). We awaken with old memories, old emotions, feelings and sensations, a compilation of neurons and synapses, biochemical reactions and energy flow that were created by all the events, thoughts, emotions, and physical reactions that we have had over our lifetime.

When I think about our mind and emotions as a filter, I'm reminded of the old *Peanuts* cartoon. There was a little boy, "Pigpen," who wasn't much for bathing. Everywhere he went, a cloud of dirt surrounded him. Each of us carries a similar cloud around with us every day. We awaken to see the world around us through the past we have accumulated—no wonder the present moment sometimes seems so foggy and frustrating!

Unlike Pigpen, we have the opportunity to "take an awareness bath." We can bathe our experiences in the cleansing power of awareness, allow preconceived notions of how we see the world and ourselves to arise and be "seen," and wash away the mental and emotional dirt we have accumulated. This is the power of simple awareness: to see ourselves and the world more clearly, beyond our preconceived thoughts and emotions.

WARNING: When we begin to practice meditation, we most likely will first see the dirt more clearly. We might see it in the form of thoughts that race through our minds and emotions that race through our bodies. Most of us probably begin meditation practice with the hope of gaining a sense of peace. The good news is that is possible and likely, *but first*, be prepared to have some moments of, "Oh, crap! That's what I've been thinking and feeling all these years? That's where I'm stuck?" We can celebrate these epiphanies and continue to bathe in the natural awareness of each moment. This "letting come and go" practice is all part of the transformation process. Trust that it is worth a little pain, grieving, and sadness to go through the shadows and find the sun shining more brightly on the other side.

A GUIDED MEDITATION TO SUPPORT NATURAL AWARENESS:

- Begin by becoming aware of whatever sensations are arising in your body. Hot? Cold? Pain? Pleasure? Where is the sensation? What exactly does it feel like? When you sit still, you can sometimes become aware of the sensation of your heart beating, or the sensation of your blood flowing through your veins.

- Then shift awareness to hearing. What does it feel like to hear? Some noises might be deemed pleasant, unpleasant, or neutral. Instead of focusing on your preference for certain sounds, cultivate a sense of curiosity about what hearing feels like, regardless of what the sound may be.

- Then shift awareness to thinking/emotions. These two activities often go hand-in-hand. A thought arises that causes an emotion, or an emotion arises that causes a thought. Look beyond or beneath the thought or emotion itself and explore what it feels like to think. What are the sensations of particular emotions? Can you catch the moment when a thought arises, or when it falls away? Practice staying present with whatever arises.

- Then shift to opening your eyes to experience seeing. What does "seeing" feel like? Is it possible to see beyond preferences and perceptions, labels and judgments?

- Then just be aware of whatever is happening internally or externally. Practice resting in awareness with curiosity and without preference or judgment.

I sometimes suffered from severe anxiety, which was one of my early motivations for learning to meditate. As I sat, I learned to feel the anxiety arising, which sometimes led to panic. Slowly, I was able to cultivate a sense of curiosity about what anxiety feels like. I shifted my experience from being afraid of it to becoming curious about it. It seemed to arise in my throat, giving way to a sense of tightness and tension, and my heart began to race. All these sensations can cause greater anxiety, but when I breathed into the feeling and tried to stay with it in as neutral a way as I could, then it more quickly dissipated. Those anxious feelings often led to anxious thoughts—"What can I do to stop this feeling?" "I'm going to be exhausted for my meeting tomorrow if this continues…" It was especially difficult if it happened in the middle of the night when I just wanted to go back to sleep. The guided meditation practice above is a great tool if you are having trouble sleeping. Sometimes I'm back to sleep before I finish.

The good news is that everyone has this innate sense of well-being within them—it is, unfortunately, often covered up by past experiences, tattered storylines, and old ways of seeking happiness in inherently dissatisfying ways. Natural awareness uncovers this amazing ability within each of us to tolerate difficult thoughts and emotions, enabling us to get beyond them and more fully enjoy each moment of living.

Chapter 10

POSITIVE IMAGERY

We each have this incredible tool of imagination within us:

1. Know that it is always available, no matter where we are or who we are with.

2. Exercise it; strengthen your use of it.

3. Rest in knowing that imagination is limitless.

4. Imagine your life as a clean sheet of paper that is waiting for the living to be written down on it, to be lived, moment by moment. In this moment, imagine

your life as a finely written novel, with you as the hero or heroine. What would you write? How would you live? What would you create anew?

Strengthening our imagination muscles lets us benefit from the practice of visualization. This is the "fake it till you make it" part that has been scientifically proven to be true. Athletes can imagine performing their physical activities and, by doing so, do a better job when they actually play their sports. We can practice feeling a certain way and we'll slowly begin to actually experience the world in this new way of being. Four qualities that are worth cultivating (because they create a greater sense of well-being) are loving-kindness, compassion, sympathetic joy, and equanimity. These four qualities can be practiced by imagining exactly how we would think, feel and act if we were having these positive mental states.

- Loving-kindness can be practiced to overcome anger and fear. This type of love is not the kind where we are expecting the other person to love us back. Instead, we radiate loving-kindness regardless of whether we have a relationship with the person or not, whether we like them or not. We can look beyond a person's unskillful words or actions and send them loving-kindness anyway. Imagine that everyone deserves to be loved, not because of what they look like or who they are or how they act, but because they are a human being.

- Compassion can be cultivated to overcome selfishness and self-centered thinking. We consider the well-being of another and wish for their well-being, as well as take action to relieve others' suffering. These practices create a positive sense of well-being in ourselves by being of service to others.

- Sympathetic joy helps us overcome resentment, hatred and jealousy. We cultivate sympathetic joy by rejoicing in the good fortune of others, and by wishing to give away our joy to all beings. All beings wish to experience joy, and we can radiate joy towards all beings, even that co-worker who annoys us or our irritating neighbor with the continuously barking dogs.

- Equanimity overcomes prejudice and bias. Equanimity is the practice of recognizing that everyone deserves loving-kindness, compassion, joy and happiness. A person may be speak and act unskillfully, but we can learn to look beyond their poor behavior and see their humanity. These practices are *not* about being a doormat. If someone is harming you, you need to take appropriate action. However, we can still radiate love and compassion, if even from afar. We are inseparably interconnected and interdependent with each other. With this knowledge, we can find love, compassion, and joy for each other, as well as for ourselves.

Initially, we may not feel loving or compassionate or joyful. Sometimes, when we try to silently wish everyone to be happy, we don't feel happy or peaceful ourselves. Just sit with whatever arises. Feel it completely, then go back to the practice of imagining feeling loving and kind. This practice is not to whitewash over longstanding emotions. Instead, it is to uproot those old habitual emotions by seeing them more clearly, even making friends with them, then replacing them with kinder and more productive ways of viewing ourselves and the world.

Let's start with a deeper definition of love, usually called loving-kindness to distinguish it from our run-of-the-mill, often experienced, lusty love—that love when we see someone or something we want. I want that person, I want that car, I want that thing. That kind of love is more like lust and greed—it usually has nothing to do with focusing on the other person's happiness unless it intersects with our own. Loving-kindness, however, is love without attachment, love without expectations. We imagine ourselves to be loving and kind in order to cause love and kindness to more naturally arise.

Next, we can explore cultivating compassion, described as an unselfish, detached emotion that gives one a sense of urgency in wanting to help others. This is not "idiot" compassion, where we feel we must over-give of ourselves and our money, which may come from our feeling a sense of lack or poverty or guilt. Compassion, in this sense, is opening up to the feeling that we are all interconnected and interdependent. Imagine that when you reach out in compassion, you are reaching out to yourself. We practice imagining walking a mile in the other person's shoes. We can learn to no longer feel the need to run away from another's pain, but to take appropriate action to help alleviate the suffering.

Third is sympathetic joy. This is the joy we experience for others when they gain. Have you ever felt jealousy or frustration instead of joy when a colleague got a raise or a new job? These unskillful reactions can lead to resentment and anger. Cultivating sympathetic joy is a way to clearly see what we're holding on to and our habitual clinging of working only for our own happiness, even at the expense of others' well-being. We practice rejoicing in the good fortune of others and also imagine giving away our own joy to others. If we are inseparably interconnected and interdependent, then we are essentially sharing joy with ourselves—the greater sense of Self.

Last is equanimity. We first practice seeing how we judge others and ourselves as better than or less than. A great exercise is to spend one day noticing how you judge yourself and others with comparisons of "like," "dislike," or "irrelevant." By bringing these judgments to the surface, you have a chance to choose differently, perhaps giving yourself and everyone the benefit of curiosity about who you/they are and getting to accept yourself and others more fully.

I was on a silent retreat, and one person pointed out that they realized that while flossing their teeth, they were feeling a sense of superiority. "I'm better than most people because I floss every day!" When they said this, I realized that I do this too. I often unconsciously judge my behaviors based on how I'm doing compared to everyone else—better than or less than or the same? Practicing equanimity helps us go beyond superficial comparisons to see the humanity in us all. Most likely, we all want and need the same thing—to feel loved and cared for. Practice looking beyond unskillful behavior and look for the good. It's there within us all, just waiting to be recognized and supported.

This practice of equanimity does *not* mean that we treat every person and every situation exactly the same. It doesn't mean that we don't take action when someone is trying to harm us or when we might be trying to harm ourselves. When we are fully present in each moment, we will see more clearly that certain situations and certain people require different reactions and responses in order to be skillful. However, we can start from a place of imagining others as just like us—everyone wants to be happy and feel loved, right? So, we practice wanting everyone, including ourselves, to be happy.

Loving kindness, compassion, sympathetic joy, and equanimity practices are a way to understand how we currently experience ourselves and others, then encourages us to explore a new way of being and feeling. What would it feel like to live life with more love, compassion, joy and happiness?

Science proves that visualizing these positive qualities actually rewires our brains over time to rest in a these mental states more often. There is a wonderful book, *Happiness,* written by Matthieu Ricard, who, through MRI technology, was shown to be the happiest man in the world. He has a far greater number of happiness synapses than anyone else ever tested. He achieved this happiness through years of visualizing these positive qualities. He chose happiness again and again, and his brain rewired itself to naturally create the experience on its own.

If you look out into a crowd, you will likely see only your friends. The others, if you see them at all, may look like stick figures. We can train ourselves to see everyone as being just like us—as someone who wants to be happy and wants to feel loved and cared for. We can still assess when we need to protect ourselves, but our ability to love will increase.

We can use positive imagery to create new neural networks for loving-kindness, compassion, sympathetic joy, and equanimity (i.e. going beyond the usual judgments of "friend," "enemy," or "stranger").

Below are some suggested positive imagery practices. You can simply record them for yourself to listen to while you close your eyes, or download them from SerenityPause.com.

HERE IS A SIMPLE GUIDED MEDITATION TO BEGIN FOCUSING ON EQUANIMITY:

We do not often think of all beings as our equals. We see their appearance, hear their words, and experience their actions. Then we judge them in a myriad of ways—better than us, less than us, etc. The following exercise strengthens our ability to see all beings as worthy of loving-kindness, compassion, sympathetic joy, and happiness. We still hold people accountable for their unskillful actions, but we first see them as human beings who want to be loved and cared for, even if they are doing so in unskillful ways.

- Close your eyes and take a few slow deep breaths, and let's begin with you. Silently and sincerely say to yourself, "I deserve to be loved. I deserve compassion. I deserve to be joyful. I deserve to be happy." Breathe in the possibility that these statements are true. What would it feel like if they were true? What arises that is in conflict with these statements? Do you think you are unlovable or undeserving? What if that weren't true? How might you show up in life differently? How might you respond to life in a different way if you knew the truth that you do deserve to be loved?

- Next, bring to mind your close friends and family. Choose one person at a time, and imagine that person in front of you in this very moment. Silently and sincerely say, "You deserve to be loved. You deserve compassion. You deserve to be joyful. You deserve to be happy." Breathe in the possibility that these are true statements. What would it feel like if they were true? What arises that is in conflict with these statements? Some people believe their friends or family members need to be punished for hurting them before they would "deserve this." What if that weren't true? It is helpful to start from a place of love and compassion. What if we began with empathy instead of disdain and judgment?

- Next, imagine it possible to bring to mind all beings on the planet and that you could look each person in the eyes, one by one. Silently and sincerely say, "You deserve to be loved. You deserve compassion. You deserve to be joyful. You deserve to be happy." Drink in that possibility. We can still protect ourselves from being harmed, but also cultivate this positive mental state to transform the way we interact with ourselves and all other beings.

- Some people have told me that this practice is unrealistic and impossible. I acknowledge that it might be difficult, but I encourage you to try anyway. I offer the recent situation (although I cannot suggest this as the safest response) of Antoinette Tuff, who works in the front office at Ronald E. McNair Discovery Learning Academy just outside Atlanta, Georgia. When confronted by a man who was ready to kill as many people as possible, she chose to see his humanity and saved many lives by connecting with him as a human who was suffering. Who knows what minor miracles we might create in our own lives (and the ripple impact on others) by starting from a place of equanimity?

Chapter 11

FIND YOUR INNER CHEERLEADER

As you practice meditation, it helps to become aware of the specific criticisms from your inner voice. After a session, try writing down whatever negative, critical thoughts arose within you. Knowing what you are telling yourself gives you a powerful opportunity to change your inner dialogue.

Instead of letting your inner drill sergeant run amok, I encourage you to find a gentler voice and a kinder image. When you realize you are distracted, celebrate with an internal, "Yay!" or touchdown dance, and then return to attention to the breath.

What would a gentle, kind voice inside your head sound like? What would it say to you? What if you had an internal cheerleader who encouraged you and said kind words about how strong, courageous, and powerful you are? Changing that voice in your head can be a transformative tool in your life.

There is a Harvard research study that discovered it is *not* the amount of stress you experience that harms you but, rather, what you tell your-self about stress that makes all the difference. Having high levels of stress and believing that stress is bad for you (that drill sergeant in your head) can make you significantly more likely to die in the next five years. *But* having a lot of stress and believing that stress is good for you, that turns out to make you less likely to die in the next five years. The positive inner voice completely erases any negative physical effect of stress. Having an encouraging inner cheerleader prepares you for the challenges of life and interprets your racing heart as pumping blood into your system to give you courage and confidence. It's not the stress that is dangerous, but our thoughts about the stress! For details, go to: http://www.ted.com/talks/kelly_mcgonigal_how_to_make_stress_your_friend.html.

I suggest that you try out different voices to find the one that resonates in your heart. It may seem goofy, but finding your internal mental trainer is a powerful tool for overcoming the varying struggles and suffering that happens in every life. It might be the voice of a trusted friend or a kind aunt or uncle. My voice sounds a lot like Ellen DeGeneres—it's funny and joking so I don't take myself too seriously, and she spontaneously dances in my head sometimes just to remind me to laugh, to savor life and find joy in each moment!

Then, find the encouraging statements that work best. Go beyond the mere superficial, like Stuart Smiley's Saturday Night Live character, "I'm good enough, I'm smart enough, and doggonit, people like me!" You might recall times in the past when you've done your best or remember the supportive words of a dear friend or a teacher or coach. As you remind yourself of these positive statements, also be aware of whatever conflicting thoughts or emotions might arise. Examine gently what the drill sergeant is saying, where is that coming from? Then reinforce the positive statement again and again, feel it in your body, let it resonate in every cell, that sense of loving and supporting yourself from the inside out.

Lastly, music can also work well for some people. Is there a song or tune that uplifts you or brings you peace and calm? Perhaps the words or the melody melt away the stress or inspire you to keep going when the going gets tough. I often hear the theme from the "Rocky" movies when I'm in a tough spot. It revs me up, and gets my blood pumping, ready to leap over tall buildings and take on the world.

Encouraging voices, statements, music—they all have the ability to create inspiration in our mind and our body, as well as to cultivate a positive state of being. These supportive sounds rewire our brains to be more resilient, flexible and creative whenever we face the inevitable challenges in life.

Chapter 12

LOOKING FOR LOVE IN ALL
THE RIGHT PLACES

"What does it matter if everybody loves me or nobody loves me? I am love, and I can be love expressing." Jeffrey Miller

I always remember that great country and western song *"Lookin' for Love"* by Waylon Jennings.

I was looking for love in all the wrong places

Looking for love in too many faces

Searching your eyes, looking for traces

Of what...I'm dreaming of...

Hopin' to find a friend and a lover

God bless the day I discover

Another heart, lookin' for love.

With positive imagery, we start to look for love in all the right places, first and most importantly, within our own hearts. Everyone has innate love within them—it might covered up by painful past experiences or over-protected due to past harms and hurts but it is still there, just waiting to be discovered, uncovered and tapped into. We can cultivate love, regardless of our situation or circumstances. With meditation and awareness, we uncover how to we might be sabotaging our loving relationships with pre-conceived notions about ourselves and about love itself.

There are three behaviors we can cultivate that are components of any loving relationship: patience, openness, and appreciation.

Let's begin with patience. How might cultivating patience also nurture a sense of love and compassion? What would patience feel like? We can cultivate patience with our family and friends, but also with strangers and even enemies. Consider how cultivating patience when you wait in line or are inconvenienced in some way might transform the experience into loving-kindness—love without clinging. Think back on this past week and consider where an application of patience might have created a different experience. When might you have been able to transform your experience of a difficult situation by cultivating patience?

Next, we can cultivate openness, by proactively recognizing the innate goodness in ourselves and in everyone, regardless of any unskillful behavior. You may not believe that everyone is innate good—it would be easy to find evidence to support that people are innately "bad" if we only used as evidence their hurtful words or actions. But, in this practice, we start by exploring being open to the possibility that people are innate good. Going further, how might we be open to others' pain and suffering, rather than simply looking for how they will make *us* feel good, or whether they might please us? We can practice being open to the possibilities for love in all situations and for all people, and being compassionately aware of what might be the most skillful behavior for us. Reflecting on this last week, can you recall a time when you might have been able to use a sense of openness to explore a more skillful response to a situation, circumstance, or relationship?

Third, we can cultivate appreciation. We can practice *not* looking for what's wrong with people, but rather looking for what's right/good/skillful—whatever words work best for you. We can catch someone doing good or being skillful or kind, and praise them for it.

At a spiritual community I attended in Dallas, the youth director reflected on how to apply this practice with children. When the kids came up on the stage each Sunday, some of them jumped off at the end instead of using the three small steps at the side. (The stage was only about three feet high but could be dangerous for a four-year old.) The youth director found himself yelling at the kids, "Don't jump off the stage!" The service ended with the frantic shout of his frustration.

He asked himself how he could achieve the same objective using patience, openness, and appreciation. At the end of each service, he began announcing that the children would now joyfully put at least one foot on each stair—how wonderful they were for their joyful marching! Eureka! It worked. Each child started to joyfully march off the stage and down the stairs. This may seem silly or unimportant, but think about the many times in our lives we focus on what people are doing wrong instead of what they are doing right. It was such a delight to see all the children cheerfully marching down the stairs, one by one.

How much time do you you spend focusing on what *you* are doing wrong instead of what you are doing right? Reflect and learn from your mistakes, but also move on, start fresh, and explore new, more skillful words and actions. When doubts arise, remember to look for the innate good that is there within us all. The good you seek is right where you are. The love you desire is already present. Experience your own worth, feel the love within you. You and I and all of us are worthy of love.

We can explore with delight, applying patience, openness, and appreciation to our cultivation of love within ourselves and in all situations.

HERE IS A GUIDED MEDITATION TO CULTIVATE LOVING-KINDNESS:

- As always, begin with some slow, full breaths. Start by visualizing someone you see as a role model for loving-kindness (someone you've known or a spiritual figure such as Jesus or Buddha, Mother Teresa or the Dalai Lama, or even just a divine spirit or your best friend— whatever image works best for you. Imagine that person giving you loving-kindness. Imagine the powerful energy of love pouring down over you like warm rays of sunshine, filling up every cell of your body with the deepest feeling of being loved and cared for, accepted just the way you are.

- Then visualize that you have within you this innate and unlimited source of loving-kindness (that unconditional love that arises from simply from the desire to be loving). Imagine sending yourself loving-kindness. You can use the silent phrase, "May I be happy" to remind yourself of this amazing source of love within you.

- Realize that you have more than enough love within you to share with others. Visualize a dear friend, or even a pet, right in front of you at this very moment, and begin sending loving-kindness ("May you be happy") without expecting anything in return.

- Replace this image with a neutral person, a stranger— perhaps the cashier at the grocery store or someone driving next to you on the road—and radiate out loving-kindness to that person as well ("May you be happy").

- Replace this image with someone you may find it difficult to be with, perhaps a coworker or family member or even someone like a criminal or a murderer. Visualize sending them loving-kindness ("May you be happy") without expecting anything in return.

- Visualize that this unlimited love within you radiates out in all directions, more than enough to share with every single being on the planet in this moment. Close the visualization with wishing for all beings, including yourself, to be happy, peaceful, and free from suffering.

- Be attentive to whatever thoughts, emotions, or sensations arise throughout the process. Imagine what it would feel like to be loving and kind and what it would feel like to radiate out an unlimited amount of loving-kindness.

Chapter 13

LIGHTEN UP!

Laughter and a sense of humor can contribute greatly to your meditation practice. Seriously, let's not take ourselves so seriously! Let's incorporate playfulness. Let's go to the park and run and skip and not worry about looking foolish. When was the last time you swung in a swing for no reason at all? Let's give each moment our all, and our "all" can be whimsical and silly.

I proclaim that another great meditation practice can be watching old Monty Python shows and movies—one can't get much sillier than that. I have laughed out loud and long watching something as simple as the *Ministry of Silly Walks*. (It's available on YouTube and still makes me laugh uncontrollably!)

Let's support and encourage ourselves and each other to play and laugh more. Imagine the possibility that a feeling of savoring life might arise a little more often.

Many of you may be aware of laughter yoga, which is as easy as laughing for no reason. You can find more detailed instructions LaughterYoga.org. It's fairly simple. Laugh. For no reason. Get together with others and agree to laugh for no reason. It actually works.

I saw a video the other day of a woman who had allegedly scored the highest on a test about how much happiness one experienced in life. When this woman was interviewed about how she achieved such a high level of happiness in her life, she mentioned three things: attitude, gratitude, and cartoons.

Chapter 14

MEDITATION FOR WEIGHT LOSS

There have been times when I have sat in front of the TV, fascinated by some movie or show, and somehow have eaten a whole bag of chips, along with some chocolate cookies and a few sodas. How did that happen? I really like chips—salt and vinegar are my favorites—and I think dark chocolate is simply the most beautiful food ever invented, one of the great joys in life. I have been known to eat while driving down the road with the radio on and talking on the phone—this is *not* safe, either physically or psychologically!

The more I meditate, the less natural it feels to eat while being distracted. These meditation practices can help transform the way we experience hunger, eating and drinking, and as a result, transform our health and happiness.

Eating with concentration and awareness is a meditation on the sensations of the entire experience. This process is not about counting calories or eating any particular type of food. Meditative eating begins with being aware of what hunger feels like. Start with understanding hunger so you know when you are really needing to eat. We often eat due to cues that have nothing to do with feeling hungry. There are external cues, such as certain times of day and certain physical locations: it's ten in the morning, so it is time for a snack. I'm in my car driving by McDonald's, so it's time for a Chicken Nuggets, or whatever your particular pattern might be. There are also internal cues that may be either about actual hunger, or about a learned habit of eating to relieve an uncomfortable emotional sensation or to numb out from difficult thoughts and situations in our lives. Sometimes, we eat because we feel badly about haven eaten too much—"this day is shot so might as well have another cupcake".

With awareness we begin by more clearly understand what triggers the desire to eat. Take three slow, deep breaths when the desire to eat arises, and ask yourself, "What is causing this desire?"

We can radically transform the way we approach eating by making a commitment to be aware of the entire eating process.

Meditative eating is also about being fully aware of how you feel when you choose the food you will eat, to be aware of seeing the food before you start to eat, and to be aware of how it feels to bite into it, chew it, and swallow it, adding the experience with beverages as well. Without trying to "go on a diet," begin with simply being aware of what your current eating and drinking cues and responses are, including what thoughts, emotions, and sensations arise as you begin to desire something, and then the thoughts, emotions and sensations that arise during the process of going to get the food or beverage, then being aware of whatever thoughts, emotions and sensations arise as you eat/drink.

Last, fully experience the thoughts, emotions, and sensations that arise *after* the process. This will give you specific information about what causes any unhealthy habits. These are the first steps in changing them.

When you eat or drink, just eat or just drink. One single, powerful change in eating habits can be to proactively decide to, as much as possible, single task. Just eat. This might seem difficult during meals with friends or family. It turns out that we often eat about 20 percent more calories when we eat with others. Try creating a five-minute quiet period when the food first arrives that gives everyone an opportunity to focus solely on eating. Try it as an experiment—you will be surprised by the difference those five minutes can make.

I have friends who have agreed to share a bit of mindful eating with each meal. We build in a five-minute period of silence so we have time to savor the experience: "Try the "one bite at a time" practice. First, look at the food, smell it, be aware of any thoughts or emotions that arise. Second, pick up one bite and put it in your mouth; be aware of the texture and flavor. Third, chew very slowly, then swallow, aware of any sensations, thoughts and emotions that might arise. This process takes more time and gives your internal cue of fullness time to register and be noticed.

When you do overeat, be fully aware of the experience afterward. What are the thoughts, emotions, and sensations of overeating? If you have a tendency, as most of us do, to beat yourself up over bad behavior, find a way to infuse learning and forgiveness. Here is a simple reflection that can help:

1. Bring to mind the specific unskillful behavior, recalled in great detail.

2. Ask yourself, "What did I learn?" See what arises. Sometimes there are answers of ridicule and shame. Go further and explore what the positive lesson might be— what triggered the unskillful behavior?

3. Silently and sincerely say, "I forgive myself." What would forgiveness feel like?

4. Ask yourself, "What will I do different going forward?" Be very specific in your answer.

5. Imagine what it would feel like to truly learn, forgive, and move forward. The imagery might be that of setting down a heavy bag of guilt and shame and walking

away from it. Be aware of what it would feel like to begin anew.

6. Finish by writing down the entire experience including the answers to these important questions.

Ice cream and chocolate are *not* the enemy. There is no enemy. Eating can become a sensual, joyful process that enriches your body and your mind without expanding your waistline and your worry.

Chapter 15

MEDITATE WITH OTHERS

You might avoid organized religion like the plague or you may have a spiritual community you enjoy and attend regularly or you might fall somewhere in the middle of this wide spectrum. The last fifty years have seen a prolific diversification in sources of spirituality and social circles. Finding a way to meditate with others does not require joining anything. It can be as simple as starting a group of like-minded people who want to meditate as well or joining a group that has already been established.

I have several friends who love to ride motorcycles and say that each Sunday they worship at the house of Harley-Davidson, as they socialize with friends who have similar interests. Some of them also love to meditate. *What?* Is it possible to love Harleys and love meditation too? Stereotypes, as we all know, are often caricatures of real human beings. We are diverse, we are complicated, and we are each unique in our own way. There has never been anyone exactly like you in the history of the world, and there never will be anyone exactly like you in the future—you can celebrate your "you-ness." In the words of Dr. Seuss: "Today you are You, that is truer than true. There is no one alive who is Youer than You."

With this in mind, let's explore how you might find a way to meditate with others that feels right for you. **There is research that validates that the vibration of people who sing together** causes their heartbeats to synchronize. Meditating together can help create this greater resonance with those around us. Meditating with others is also a great source of inspiration and encouragement.

Here are some options:

FIND A MEDITATION GROUP THAT ALREADY MEETS. Just like Weight Watchers helps people lose weight together, making meditation a habit is easier if you have a group of like-minded people who will meditate with you. It can be as simple as Googling "meditation groups" in your area, or signing up for Meetup.com, which is a great, a free source for finding like-minded individuals with a variety of interests. (There's even a Meetup group for people who like to pole dance as a form of exercise—it's possible there are some meditators among them...who knows?)

START YOUR OWN GROUP. You might decide to start your own meditation group. It can be as simple as having a sitting group in your home once a week, or starting a meditation group at your yoga center, health club, church, temple, or office. Meditation is now a part of the Pentagon's program for officers, while military hospitals are exploring meditation as a treatment for post-traumatic stress syndrome. In some cases, they find meditation to be more effective than drug treatments. (Wired magazine, December 2013).

Here's an easy way to set up a meditation group near you:

- **Find a location.** Find a place that is consistently available at whatever time you decide to meet. You can start in your home, but that can become difficult if you publicly promote your group. Many offices buildings, yoga centers, health clubs, churches, and temples allow meditation groups to meet if they make a small donation and will even advertise your group in their newsletters or bulletin boards.

- **Find a co-leader.** Choose someone you can trust to lead the group when you cannot be there. Consistency is key for a meditation group to flourish. Having two people to share leadership (which includes showing up when the group meets and getting things started) increases the likelihood of a group's success.

- **Be patient.** In 1999, I returned from my first meditation retreat so excited that I wanted to share this amazing practice with anybody who was interested (while trying not to be a meditation televangelist). Together with my friend, Bruce Nelson, a long-time meditator, we formed a meditation group focused on the basic meditation techniques described in chapter four. For our initial meeting, we had twenty people—yahoo! With that initial success, we decided to meet every other Saturday. The first year, we had two to six people show up, and sometimes it was just Bruce and me. I encourage you to continue to hold the space through the early months— it takes time to build a meditation group membership. Don't get discouraged when no one shows up—meditate anyway.

  I am proud to report that our group still meets. Fifteen years later, the group has about twenty-five people who come together every other week. There have also been two couples who found each other through the group and are now married—what a great side benefit of meditation.

- **Promote it.** You can promote your group in a variety of ways. We began with flyers that we distributed at the local Starbucks and other various restaurants and cafés. We created a one-page website with all the information. Now we are blessed with the ability to use Facebook,

Twitter, Instagram, and Pinterest—there are many free social media options to promote your group. Meetup.com has a small charge to set up a group, but we found it to be well worth it. Meetup.com e-mails people in your area who have already expressed an interest in meditation or similar activities. You can also check SerenityPause.com to see if there is a group near you, and if you use this meditation technique, we will promote your group on our website.

- **Let us help.** You do not have to be a meditation expert to start a group. There are many wonderful downloadable meditation instructions and guided meditations to help lead you. Here's a shameless plug for SerenityPause.com. There are meditations that range from fifteen to thirty minutes. You'll also find many free meditation lessons at templebuddhistcenter.blogspot.com. My personal mission is to make it easy for anyone anywhere to learn meditation and experience the well-documented benefits.

- **Hold the meeting.** Prepare the room at least fifteen minutes in advance with chairs or mats and cushions. You might decide to invest in a good bell, if you like the bell thing.

- **Consider additional options.** Helping the group get to know each other helps bond each person to the process. I try to find out everyone's name, and you might consider having nametags with a marker to make it easier to remember each other.

For more advanced meditation techniques, you can also be certified as a Serenity Pause Meditation Leader. More information is available at serenitypause.com.

Chapter 16

MEDITATE WITH FAMILY

Having been a wife as well as a single working mom, I know firsthand the struggles of finding five seconds, much less five minutes, in a day to do anything other than fix meals, go to work, chauffeur the kids around, and do laundry. What I found easiest was combining the meditative practices with some of these activities. Our partners and children have the same issues we have—being distracted by the myriad of technologies that have invaded our lives along with all the other activities that need to get done in any given day. Sharing this practice with our families can create a greater bond and a common language for dealing with the stress and struggles that inevitably arise.

With our partners, we can start with the possibility that they will meditate with us. This might seem natural and easy or might be absolutely impossible to imagine. My dear partner who passed away four years ago intellectually understood the value of meditation, but was never willing to give it a try. I loved him anyway. And he was always supportive of me taking time out to sit in silence. One way to ease into the process is to combine meditation with other activities you do together. Could you spend five minutes together eating with awareness in silence? Perhaps there could be some concentrated clothes folding or chore doing? Even agreeing to spend five minutes each day focused solely on communicating with each other might be a great start. Find any tiny bridge that opens the conversation to the possibility of building in a few meditative moments with your partner each day. You may still have to go it alone, but at least you will have tried.

Teaching our children meditative skills gives them a precious gift that can benefit them for a lifetime. It will help them with self-regulation and confidence-building. Teaching children to meditate is a book in and of itself (for a great one, I recommend Peggy Mulvihill's *Calm Kids*). Briefly, I encourage you to set aside five minutes each day with your child(ren) to build these powerful skills of concentration, awareness, and positive imagery. Below are some simple methods to try.

Singing bowls are an easy practice that can be engaging for younger children. You can purchase small singing bowls online or in many different stores. A singing bowl is struck with a mallet, and the sound lingers for a few moments. Simply ask the children to raise their hands the second they can no longer hear the sound of the bowl.

At mealtime, you can also ask younger children to describe what their food looks like, what it tastes like, what it feels like to chew and swallow. This practice enables them to pay closer attention to the experience and helps develop language skills.

Consider using art with older children as a way of exploring positive imagination. Begin by first helping them understand the power of their imaginations to create a positive experience, regardless of their external circumstances. Then describe the positive qualities of loving-kindness, compassion, sympathetic joy, and wishing happiness for others. Have them choose one of these qualities and draw a picture that expresses the feeling they get when they feel that positive feeling. Older children often like to make up characters that display these positive qualities by writing and drawing their own storybooks.

For teenagers, well…

Some teenagers think meditation is cool and may give it a try for that reason alone. I've had some luck having high school students visualize the loving-kindness practice, or explore the sensations in their bodies. It might be easier to explain the skills themselves or find a teachable moment one on one.

In the heat of an argument with my daughter, neither of us usually were very skillful with these practices. We just had to walk away for a few minutes or hours. Most importantly, I found that when I would slow down my own breathing and imagined radiating out peace and calm, it change the environment of the entire situation. This process also gave me time (the wonderful gap...) to be more aware of what I was thinking or feeling. After we both had time cooled down, sometimes it was possible to circle back around and ask her about her experience of what happened, in as neutral way as possible. I often found that if I could start apologizing for my own unskillful behavior, it opened the door for her to be willing to explore what she had said or done that might have been hurtful. Being a role model for our children is the most powerful tool for them to learn these life skills.

As parents, we can practice our loving skills of patience, openness and appreciation, balanced with clear intentions and boundaries. Our actions speak louder than our words. Some days, I felt like I was doing a great job as a mom, and all was right with the world. On other days, I struggled mightily, and everything I did seemed to be wrong. Sometimes I was simply grateful when the day was done, so I could start fresh tomorrow. Perhaps now is a good time to talk about gratitude.

Chapter 17

THE POWER OF GRATITUDE AND GENEROSITY

An extensive amount of research has been done on the power of practicing gratitude and generosity. Exercising our gratitude and generosity muscles greatly increases an experience of peace and happiness in many aspects of our life.

First we can create simple ways of identifying what we are grateful for. Consider creating a gratitude journal. Each morning, identify five positive things (people, situations, actions, learnings, outcomes, experiences) and write one sentence about them. As reported in a *New York Times* article, Professors Robert A. Emmons and Michael E.

McCullough created an experiment to study the power of gratitude. One group of people created a simple gratitude journal. After two months, the gratitude group reported feeling happier and more optimistic than the control group. *They also spent more time working out and had fewer physical problems.* Something as simple as being more aware of the things that are good in our lives can build our confidence to choose healthier behaviors in other areas of our lives at the same time.

Our family always took time before our Thanksgiving meal to offer one thing we were grateful for. Some family members struggled to think of anything. At least one of the kids would say, "Pumpkin pie." (Aren't we all grateful for that?) Others would dig deep to find a positive quality in a family member with whom they had difficulty. Start where you are. It doesn't have to be about curing cancer. It can be something as simple as the fact that someone smiled at you today, or a helpful stranger held the door open when you needed it.

Generosity is another way to transform our experiences of ourselves and the world around us. Regardless of the amount of money in our bank account, we can find a myriad of ways to be generous with our time and our talents. Serving others is a proven method for creating more happiness in our lives (see Martin Seligman's book, *Flourish*, for quantitative studies and details).

Serving others can be deeply rewarding and uncomplicated. Work at the soup kitchen in your town, tutor a child in reading, set aside a volunteer day where you and your family together help out in the community. Be generous with a supportive word or some encouragement to your friends and coworkers.

Want to really freak people out? Offer someone the chance to cut ahead of you in line at the bank or grocery store. Pay for coffee for the person in line behind you. These simple acts of generosity create tidal waves of positivity that change the way you see yourself and the way you see others, and the way others see themselves. Small daily acts of generosity build up to a lifetime of happiness and joy.

Chapter 18

FROM JUDGMENT TO JOY

People often start meditating to relieve stress, and that is a wonderful result. *But*, as meditation creates a quieter external environment, this quiet time can bring more awareness to our internal environment—which is sometimes an internal cacophony of frenetic thoughts, good and bad fantasies, unruly emotions, and a myriad of good and bad sensations. We most likely were having all these thoughts, emotions, and sensations before, but we may not have consciously recognized them. Meditation can sometimes feel like suddenly being in the middle of a hailstorm, being bludgeoned by our thoughts, emotions and sensations. However, in the midst of the storm, we can hold our seat and stay with whatever arises. Don't let a few storms and bad internal weather deter you from finding your true happiness.

We incorporate the practice of concentration and awareness to weather the storm of our varying thoughts, emotions, and sensations. We cultivate awareness of them, like clouds in the sky, or like a movie we are watching, while slowly disentangling our personal identification with them. We are *not* our thoughts; we are *not* our emotions and we *not* our sensations. At the depths of our being, there is always peace and calm to be found—that is the place we can discover and return to again and again. As we return our attention to the breath, a sense of peace can be found beneath and beyond all the internal chaos.

It seems that conflict may be part of our evolutionary process. We fight when we are afraid. We fight when we aren't aware of the possibility of peaceful responses. We may also fight out of habit. Now we can challenge the notion that we are inherently angry or at odds with the world. We may get angry, but that does not have to mean that we are the anger. In the gap created by awareness, we get a precious opportunity to explore all the alternative solutions to any problem we might be facing.

If you currently hold the assumption that human beings are inherently fighters, imagine if that were not true. What if we realized and tapped into an innate ability to find peaceful solutions to whatever conflict arose? Imagine the possibilities. However, I want to add an important caveat. I understand that there are times when aggressive tactics must be taken. You might be able to save the lives of two hundred people by killing one person, and that might do the greatest good, but violence and aggression are not always the best solution. I only offer that we often rush to judgment that aggression is always the best solution.

If natural peacefulness is our birthright, how might we reclaim the experience and find a way to respond in kinder, more skillful ways?

First, **we can decide to have a larger motivation than simply the comfort of our own minds.** Focusing solely on our own personal desires and distractions at the exclusion of others often leads to unskillful words and actions. We can become more intentional in our motivations. Ask yourself, "Do I want to be a better person? Do I want to be stronger, kinder, wiser, and more focused? Am I willing to give up some old, unskillful habits to see the bigger picture and to be of greater service to myself and to the world?"

A meditation master recently said that if we put feeling peaceful above all other experiences, then we would not get much done. This might seem to be the opposite of what meditation is about. Yet, sometimes tolerating the uncomfortable is exactly what enables us to do great good, and meditation can train our minds to tolerate being uncomfortable. We can look beyond our desire to simply make ourselves—our minds, our emotions, our sensations—comfortable and, instead, expand our motivation to greater good.

As discussed in an earlier chapter, we all need to be clear about our motivations and intentions in order to get through the dark nights of the spirit when difficult times arise. Are you willing to shift your priorities so that the simple comfort of your own mind is no longer your first priority? Can you imagine the possibility of a deeper happiness that arises from being a beneficial presence and from helping to change the world, even if it requires letting go of a little peace and comfort now and then?

We all know the feeling of giving in to the fleeting thoughts and emotions we have. It's like having an allergy to a certain food and eating it anyway, so desperately wanting that initial sense of pleasure that comes from the taste and the texture, but later experiencing the allergic reaction that causes us great suffering. I am allergic to dairy—I get terrible migraines after eating it, but I absolutely *love* cheese. There are times I just want to smell, savor, and taste a glorious piece of cheese. Sometimes, usually later in the evening, the desire wears me down and I ignore the fact that in exchange for those few moments of great pleasure, I will have great suffering that will last for hours, if not days…and with a desire for immediate mental relief, I eat the cheese.

We can choose to be aware of the desire for those things that are unskillful and harmful, learn instead to tolerate the cravings, and then refocus our energies on the experience of awareness that can ultimately dissolve unskillful thinking and emotions. I am learning to tolerate the desire for cheese but not give in to the action…most of the time.

Two things that often increase the likelihood of this type of mental or emotional allergic reaction are *expectations and preferences.*

Our culture often encourages us to have high expectations. We think we must decide in advance precisely what we want, and then feel disappointed, unhappy, and discouraged when we don't get exactly that. What caused the expectation in the first place? Is it necessary to have expectations? You might find it valuable to reflect on these questions. We can explore the possibility of practicing being so present in the moment that we don't need to know exactly how things will turn out. We can head in the direction of our dreams without being so narrow-minded about exactly how we want things to turn out in life. Through practicing concentration, awareness and positive imagery, we discover what happens when we show up fully in each moment and with an intention of kindness.

Then there are the preferences we have about almost everything. When we meet people, we immediately, and sometimes subconsciously, assess their abilities to please us or annoy us or, heaven forbid, do neither. We have food, clothes, and people preferences plus so many more. We go through the world sorting everything into three categories: "I like," "I don't like," or "I ignore." Strong preferences color our experience of whatever is happening in each moment. In meditation, *we practice replacing the need for preferences with a sense of curiosity.* We learn to get comfortable with not needing everything to be a certain way.

I am a neat freak and I like my outer environment to be a certain way. (I prefer to think of it as being very "Zen." It sounds so much more pleasant) When a dear friend of mine comes to visit, she has an *entirely* different perspective of "clean enough" and finds my "Zen" habits annoying. So we both compromise. Every time I feel unhappy with my less than spick-and-span surroundings, I explore not needing things to be exactly the way I want them to be. What preferences am I willing give up in order to have her friendship and presence in my life? Is it really that important to clean everything in the house? Sometimes the answer might be yes. Other times, not so much.

Little by little, while sitting in meditation, more joy arises for "no external reason." There is joy and happiness within you right now, just waiting to be unleashed. Through the cultivation of curiosity and non-preference, we give greater joy and happiness room to expand. Let that joy and happiness within you come out and play.

Chapter 19

ADDICTIONS AND AFFLICTIONS

Here are some additional practices to untangle the power that we give to unskillful thoughts, emotions, and actions. We've all heard that our thoughts create our realities. So how can we change what we think in order to change the way we experience ourselves and the world? We can strengthen and experience our innate sense of happiness and well-being, which is beyond our thoughts, emotions, and external circumstances.

As we explore these practices in changing our thinking, we can look at some helpful research in the field of addiction recovery. *Craving to Quit,* an excellent psychiatric study by Brewer, Elwafi, and Davis, details the positive impact that awareness training can have on eliminating unskillful behavior. The study outlines three contributors to addictive behaviors:

1. **Over-rumination:** when our mind keeps repeating the same negative thoughts or storylines over and over again.

2. **Internal sensations:** those uncomfortable feelings that we either try to run away from or wallow in.

3. **External cues:** specific past events that were pleasurable or painful. We mentally associate addictive behaviors with people, times, places, even smells, and sounds. These associations create an increased desire to repeat the unskillful behavior.

Through concentration and awareness, we can practice uncoupling cravings and aversions from our reactions to them. We can learn to develop a *tolerance* for craving and aversion. We can become aware of unskillful thoughts, emotions, and automatic behaviors, and then simply watch them rather than being sucked into responding in old, habitual, unskillful ways. The three components of meditation—concentration, awareness, and positive imagery—can be powerful tools for recognizing the moment a desire to respond in unskillful ways arises and increasing our ability to explore more skillful responses, then reinforce the more skillful responses and build them into new healthy habits.

We have many opportunities to practice every day. We can practice in a controlled environment, like our focused meditation time, *and,* equally powerful, we can practice in the moment an afflictive thought or emotion arises. **It is powerful to practice in the eye of the storm.** When the unskillful thought arises, explore what healthier responses you might have—instead of a drink or a cigarette, you call a friend or your sponsor. Meditative practices give you the chance to be aware when it first starts happening, then stop, assess and choose differently. With time, these skills become your new default mode of simply being present to whatever is arising and responding a new helpful ways.

In the article on addiction, Brewer emphasizes that a powerful step toward happiness is **realizing that our thoughts and emotions only have power over us because we give it to them.** If we try to merely distract ourselves from them or ignore them, we might find temporary relief, but we are not getting to the core, the source of the suffering—and this is why many addiction recovery processes fail. The source of the suffering is that we narrowly focus on the short-term payoff that we will get from the unskillful behavior. Even though we know the long-term results are disastrous, we become enchanted, some would say obsessed, with getting that short-term feeling of relief or elation or pleasure or numbness or confidence or validation. The good news is that we can learn to become **disenchanted** with these afflictive thoughts and emotions themselves by no longer focusing on solely the short-term payoff. When you realize that you have the power within you to see through them and beyond them, then you can decide to take away the power you have given to them.

Be aware of the power you give to certain thoughts. Recognize that there is a better way of dealing with them. Recognize and reinforce that change is possible (here is a good use for your inner cheerleader). Then you can practice having a sense of **curiosity** about what these thoughts and emotions really are. Being curious about them turns out to work much more effectively than trying to beat them down or wallow in them.

The example that Brewer uses is that we have choices in our lives: to continue banging our head against the wall because that is what we have always done, *or* realize we can do something positive, like cultivating loving-kindness and peace, starting with ourselves. Another method of dissolving the power of unskillful thoughts is to find ways to serve others instead of myopically focusing on ourselves. One practice that works well in Alcoholics Anonymous is giving a newly sober person the job of making the coffee or setting out the chairs—a simple job that serves others. How might you serve others to get beyond your limited ways of thinking? With this new understanding, we then practice, again and again. Through consistent practice, we **strengthen** the mental muscle of choosing the more skillful path. We are actually rewiring our brains.

When experiencing the intense pain of addiction, Matthieu Ricard, the author of *Happiness: A Guide to Developing Life's Most Important*

Skill, encourages us to use a visualization of the ocean. Imagine soaring above the ocean of addictive thoughts and emotions, instead of being caught in a boat on the surface, in the midst of the storm. We can learn to disentangle ourselves from our thoughts, emotions, and sensations through this simple visualization that lifts us up from the stormy waves of our internal turmoil.

Chapter 20

BREAKING BAD HABITS

I'm sure we can all relate to how we get hooked in life—when we know that what we are thinking or feeling is irrational, but we can't shake it and end up responding unskillfully. It can feel yucky or sticky, like having an itch you must scratch or you'll die. Addiction is an example of getting hooked in that way.

We can also get hooked in smaller moments, when we get hooked into old habits and emotions that are triggered by situations or something someone says that make you tighten inside. It is often pre-verbal, a sensation within you like a tightening at the pit of your stomach. Then, the thoughts come flying in, and the intense desire arises to respond in an unskillful, habitual way. Think of a time when you've been criticized by someone. Recall the exact moment when something negative was said about you. What did that feel like?

The awareness practices help us wake up in the moment we get hooked, and instead of plugging into old fears and habits, we can choose to create *the gap*. Choose to rest in awareness to find a better response. *Or* if we're already fueling the unskillfulness, we can practice pulling the plug. Here are some questions to ask that create an opportunity to respond differently:

- What do you fear most? Why? How is that serving you?

- What old habits are you still thinking/saying/doing that aren't serving your greater good?

The cartoon characterization of the angel and the devil can sometimes play out in our heads. As we discussed earlier, we can choose to have a positive, helpful, supportive voice in our heads, our internal cheerleader, to transform our interpretation of thoughts, emotions, sensations, and actions. We have the ability to energize the inner cheerleader and quiet the inner critic.

To break hurtful habits, make the commitment to energize your inner cheerleader, to be aware when you have that tightening in your gut and be aware when negative thoughts and emotions arise. Pull the plug and no longer allow that inner critic to have free rein.

We can forego that short term sense of pleasure and trade it in for a longer term sense of well-being and happiness:

- **Identify the positive result you're getting from the unskillful behavior.** Part of natural awareness is discovering how our fears and unskillful behaviors are serving us. There is always some positive effect, even if it is short-term. If we overeat, we might remember the immediate relief that comes from doing so. If we get angry, we want that sense of relief from when we first strike back. **A major part of awareness is looking for the short-term payoff.** Only then can we train ourselves to choose differently.

Right now, take a specific example of a bad habit you are trying to stop. Bring to mind a recent situation where the desire to respond in that unskillful way was so strong that you decided to follow through with it. What did that desire initially feel like right before you responded? What was the payoff that you imagined and received? Psychologically, it is often described as some sense of relief. I can't stop thinking about smoking that cigarette or yelling at my sister or getting angry in traffic, until I give in and then feel some relief from my suffering. Awareness enables us to catch ourselves in that moment when we are fantasizing about the good feeling we will get from doing the unskillful thing. When we catch ourselves having those unskillful thoughts, we are more likely to avoid the unskillful action. Replace the thought and emotion about the short-term payoff with a different thought about the long-term good of a skillful response.

- **We can trust in our innate wisdom.** Find the strength that is within you to change—it's within every single person. If you constantly tell yourself how bad you are for having these unskillful reactions, you are strengthening your inner drill sergeant. Trust that you are innately good, that there is good within each and every one of us, and that we each have an enormous amount of energy and power that we can focus with laser-like precision to change the way we respond. I work in a spiritual center that has the largest Alcoholics Anonymous group in the city. I know dozens of recovering alcoholics and addicts who had been abandoned by their families and friends as completely unsalvageable, and many have found the power within themselves (and through the strength of the group support and process of AA) to transform their lives into not just a good life, but into joyful sober living. It is possible! One of my AA friends has even transformed the first step of the twelve-step program to be an affirmation. Every day he awakes and tells himself, "Today I choose to be joyfully sober."

- **H.A.A.L.T.** There's an easy acronym that some of you may have heard, H.A.A.L.T. Halt. I learned this years ago when I was reacting in irresponsible ways, and I'm amazed at how helpful it has been. H.A.A.L.T. stands for Hungry, Angry, Anxious, Lonely, Tired. Whenever these feelings arise within us, we can see them as signposts, reminders to *halt*, pause, *create a gap*, and consider carefully whether we want to act upon our urges in that moment.

My first job was working at a McDonald's Restaurant, and one of the most important things I learned was that I didn't want to be around people who were hungry. Hungry people can often be completely irrational! When I see these symptoms coming on in myself, I remember H.A.A.L.T. and then I pause, take a deep breath, and ask, "Is this really how I want to respond in this situation?"

Chapter 21

WHO ARE YOU?

I spent many years of my life trying to do only two things: make money and get promoted. During that time, I had few real friends. When I realized that my life wasn't working, I wanted to be a better friend so that I could have better friends. In short, I wanted people to like me. What I discovered was that looking externally for signals about who I should be in order to be liked led me down many wrong paths and unnecessary detours.

When I began studying and practicing meditation, I realized that the "truth" of who I am resides in my inner wisdom, beyond the preconceived notions that our culture may give me and beyond past experiences that often form a storyline about who I think I am in this moment. When I am fully present in each moment, I can be fully aware of who I am and know what is needed to be a beneficial presence. This is the power of the meditative practice.

Most of us hold on to old ideas about who we are and what we are like. We also often carry the baggage of our parents' view of the world and of us. Meditation helps peel away the layers of misunderstandings and misconceptions. Meditation helps us "see" ourselves and the world around us more clearly.

There is a book by Dan P. McAdams on narrative psychology, entitled *The Stories We Live By: Personal Myths and the Making of the Self.* He describes identity as a personal myth we create in order to construct a sense of meaning, unity, and purpose in our lives. He argues that we consciously or unconsciously compose a narrative that integrates our 1) remembered past, 2) our perceived present, and 3) our anticipated future in a way that illustrates essential truths about ourselves.

This is what many of us do. We make up stories to fill in the blanks of the things we don't really know. We look at life from the lens of our past experiences and look for reinforcement of what we already think is true.

"It's not what you look at that matters, it's what you see."—Henry David Thoreau.

It is a choice, conscious or unconscious, that we allow ourselves to be influenced by our past experiences or by what others tell us to be true. There was an economic downturn a few years ago—people lost their jobs and their homes. Yes, that is true, but each of us had a choice with what we did with that information, how we processed the information around us, and how *we* responded to what was happening. On Wall Street, it is a common understanding that bad news is infectious. In stocks, a lie can be just as damaging as the truth.

Interestingly, this phenomenon is not new. Researchers have documented that women at the turn of the twentieth century commonly reported a specific set of symptoms, including leg paralysis, temporary blindness, and facial tics. These symptoms happened to fit the well-publicized and accepted definition of something called "hysteria." Researchers found that "patients unconsciously try to produce symptoms that will correspond to the medical diagnostics of the time," Shorter explains. "This sort of cultural molding of the unconscious happens imperceptibly and follows a large number of cultural cues that patients simply are not aware of."

What stories do you tell yourself that forms your experiences of living? Imagine the possibility that you can discover your inner wisdom and then choose how you want live. Every single one of us has this incredible power within us. What if your life going forward from this moment was a blank sheet of paper? What would it be like to get comfortable with uncertainty, allow life to unfold and begin making decisions that may not be based on your old way of thinking?

How can we have the courage to examine the stories that we tell ourselves, try and see them more clearly, and let go of the need for a story at all? What are the stories that we make up about ourselves, our families, our partners, our friends, and our enemies? Some things are unchangeable, but regardless, choosing how to perceive a situation is *always* changeable. This is the powerful tool of curiosity and non-preference.

"Whenever something negative happens to you, there is always a deep lesson concealed within it."—Eckhart Tolle

Each of us can have the courage to question the stories that we have made up and, in doing so, we might feel the fear of uncertainty that arises when we don't know. If we don't have our stories, what do we have? Who are we without our stories? The truth is, that if we can sit with not knowing, our worlds can be enriched with the fullness of possibilities. We can become courageous choosers by examining our stories, embracing our fears, making friends with not knowing, and go forward with a sense of curiosity and non-preference. We can let go of our stories by being open to the question, and then courageously choose more skillful responses.

Chapter 22

BURNED POPCORN

Here is a process that might help cut through the old stories and negative self-talk that may no longer serve you. I call it "Burned Popcorn."

This simple analogy can help us examine how we interpret ourselves and the world around us. Most of us can relate to the distinct components of the burned popcorn experience. However, we can also use this analogy to break down the exact way we process what is happening inside and around us each and every moment of every day.

To begin, we can break down our experiences into five general categories:

1. **Form:** Burned popcorn begins with a form—you can hold the blackened puffed kernel in your hand and feel its texture and temperature. We experience ourselves and the world around us in this same way. It seems that each person and thing is distinct and separate, but if we were able to see everything at the atomic level, we would see mostly space with energy whirling around in it.

   Form is mostly a construct that we create in our minds in order to make sense of the world. For example, if you ate the burned popcorn, you would digest and absorb it into your system. At what point does the burned popcorn stop being popcorn and start being you? We truly are what we eat. Or rather, what we ate becomes who "we" are. Who and what you are is a composite of what you take in and what you put out.

   Try not being so sure about the separation between you and the burned popcorn (or anything or anyone that is "outside" of you). By cultivating awareness, you can cultivate a sense of being inseparably interconnected and interdependent with all things.

2. **Sensations:** The burned popcorn creates a smell, a sensation that we experience. Sensations are physical reactions

to stimuli. At this moment, you are experiencing the temperature of your location. It might seem hot, cold, or neutral to you based on how your body interprets the experience. There might be the sensation of hearing the sounds all around you. What does it feel like to hear? You might feel sleepy or restless. If you sit still, you might become aware of the sensation of your heart beating or the blood flowing through your veins. There are many sensations that arise moment by moment, many of which we are unaware of. These sensations are merely the biochemical interactions of the physical stimuli around us. We are not ourselves hot or cold—there is an experience of hot or cold (or all the other sensations) arising.

3. **Perceptions:** You may perceive the popcorn as "burned" based on your past experiences with burned popcorn. Perceptions are the concepts we create to organize the world within us and around us. As a child, you might have pointed to things and asked, "What is that?" Your parents would say a word, and you associated that word with that form or experience or sensation. If you pointed to a ball, and your parents told you it was a horse, you would associate the word *horse* with round objects. When my daughter was a child, her favorite uncle told her funny stories. One day, she held a raisin in her hand and asked, "Uncle Mike, what is this?" Dear Uncle Mike told her, "Oh, that is a cockroach...we love to eat cockroaches don't we?" The next day, my daughter went to

school and shared with her kindergarten teacher that her uncle had fed her cockroaches for dinner. That took a little explaining to avoid a visit from social services.

We label the world around us to make it easier to navigate through the complexities of life, but sometimes these perceptions lead us to wrong conclusions and cause us unnecessary suffering. When we become more aware of our perceptions, we get a chance to choose more skillfully which labels are useful and which ones are not.

4. **Mental States:** Ellen DeGeneres says, "Why not stop judging people by their sexual preferences? Let's love everyone and simply judge people by the cars they drive." We create judgments and opinions about ourselves, about others, and about the world around us. It's the same with burned popcorn. Most people judge it to be inedible, but I have a friend who *loves* burned popcorn. She becomes giddy with delight when someone burns the popcorn because she knows no one else will want it.

Based on our past experiences and the input we get from our friends and families, we put everything into three categories: wanted, unwanted, or irrelevant. By sorting each experience into one of these categories, we begin the process of trying to get more of what we want, avoid that which we don't want, and ignore everything else. This constant rearranging of everything takes a lot of energy as we try to create a world solely of our liking.

5. **Consciousness:** We now have a memory of burned popcorn that will arise whenever a similar experience occurs in the future. We will make assumptions and have preconceived notions about what we should think, say, and do. If you believed the person who burned the popcorn was being inconsiderate, then you are likely to rush to judge others in the future who make the same mistake. It happens automatically when a sight, smell, sound, or taste reminds us of past experiences. Meditation makes us aware of how these past experiences are showing up in the present moment thoughts and emotions, so we can ask ourselves, **"What will create the most good and ease the most suffering in this moment right now?"**

Who or what are you beyond these five categories? Can you imagine or experience a sense of awareness that is beyond doing and not doing, beyond thinking of "me" versus "them?" Simply resting in awareness—no place to go, nothing to fix or change, beyond any concept of self—can be a powerful practice.

Beyond our limited sense of "self," we can experience our essence as a part of the whole. As scary as this might sound, we can let go of holding on to old limiting ways of seeing ourselves. Beyond our physical beings, some believe there are spiritual selves. Whatever your beliefs might be, these practices will help you reflect upon who you think you are and what is most important in your life.

With these tools, we have an opportunity to radically shift our experiences of ourselves and the world. By being aware of what is actually happening moment by moment, we train our minds to rest in a more natural state, free from these preconceived notions and old stories. It is in our mind's nature to build concepts, apply labels and judgments, to create stories, and to have preferences. We spend our entire lives creating these comfortable boxes for ourselves. Sometimes the world messes with our boxes or the ways in which we see ourselves or the way in which we want to see ourselves. Or crappy stuff happens and makes our boxes fall apart, which is not necessarily a bad thing.

Know that you can deconstruct these old self concepts and explore new ways of being and doing. Imagine cultivating a sense of curiosity about yourself and about life. Imagine the possibility that not knowing, not being so sure, could be a place where you hang out and actually begin to enjoy. We can learn to ride the wave of living with ease and grace. Even if it seems scary at first, we can learn to embrace the uncertainty of life, ride the wave of openness and curiosity, and live life more fully because of it.

Chapter 23

WHY STIR THINGS UP?

You probably decided to buy a book on meditation to find greater peace and calm, and that is a lovely side effect of this practice. But I also encourage you to stir things up a bit. What? Aren't we trying to settle the dirt in the glass by stopping all the shaking up we normally do?

When you first start to meditate, it might **become painfully clear how many thoughts and emotions are constantly arising.** When I tell people I teach meditation, many shake their heads in despair and say, "Oh, I tried meditating...I can't do it...I think too much!" I can relate to that experience. Meditation still sometimes feels *less* peaceful rather than more agitated. But, the happiness and peace I experience is still far greater than I previously thought possible.

So, yes, we sit, concentrate and be aware, but sometimes that is too painful or too difficult a place to start. That is why we can also use some doing, like walking meditation and positive imagery, to give us time to reflect and better understand what is going on inside us. Take this precious opportunity to consider deconstructing the house of defense mechanisms and rationalizations that your mind has spent a lifetime creating.

Several years ago, I met a guy I immediately took a dislike to. I couldn't quite put my finger on it, but something about him didn't sit right with me. At first I thought it was my intuition—"I'm on to you, buster." When others commented on how nice he was, I'd become even more irritated. It took me six months to figure out what it was that bothered me—he looked almost exactly like my sister's first husband. No wonder I disliked the guy. I had to admit that I wasn't seeing him for who he really was. I had to reflect on what was going on inside of me, the stories, defenses and rational-izations, in order to remove the veil of my past experience that was not serving me in this situation.

Forgive and remember: In addition to simply sitting in the silence with awareness, we take on these additional practices to identify and then take the charge out of old memories and unskillful habits. There is a balance to be found between wallowing in our "stories" about how we have been wronged and pretending that nothing ever hurt us. Not too loose and not too tight. We practice finding the balance between these two extremes of clinging to and aversion from, to find a place where we can forgive and remember. What did I learn? What will I do differently in the future? Then, we can practice letting go and moving on...even if it takes a few days or weeks or months or years to more fully let certain memories arise and simply fall away without the unskillful response and resistance that so often entangles us.

As a mother, I had many times when I did not do my best. I had to examine those times when I was unskillful and selfish. When I began to meditate and woke up a bit, I wanted to make amends for my unskillfulness, particularly with my daughter. I wanted to give her the best that life had to offer—as I saw it.

One decision I made was to send her to an all-girls Catholic high school even though she had gone to public school up to that point.

The Catholic high school had an outstanding curriculum, and I knew my daughter would benefit since she didn't really like school. Looking back, I understand that girls in Catholic schools have all grown up with each other, have gone to church with each other, and all know each other's families...often are each other's families... and here I was a raising my daughter in a progressive "church", far different than the Catholic structure and belief system. Needless to say, she was mortified at my decision and fought me mightily for two years, confident that she would change my mind and she would get to go back to public school with her friends.

But I held my ground, thinking it was the right thing to do. After a couple of years, she settled in and tried to make new friends, which turned out to be a lot more difficult than she expected. Never asked to parties, never included in weekend events—she had a tough go of it.

One Saturday afternoon, the girls finally invited her to the mall and offered to pick her up. She was delighted and excited. She ran upstairs and primped for an hour, getting her hair and clothes "just right." She came down to the kitchen so she would be ready when they arrived. A few minutes went by, then an hour, then... they never came. She was deeply hurt and cried all night long. As a mother, I was devastated—I was the one who had put her in this situation. It was such a painful memory for me that I couldn't bear to mention it for many years afterward.

Years later, as my daughter blossomed into this fine, confident young woman, we talked about how she had so many great friends and how proud I was of who she had become. I brought up that terrible day so I could apologize for having put her through that. She said she had always considered it the best thing that could have happened to her. "What?" I asked. She said, "That day, I made a commitment to myself that I would never make anyone else feel like that." Here is an example of the value in stirring things up, reflecting on what happens to us in life, and deciding for ourselves how to respond to each and every situation, whether it is a wonderful experience or whether it is a horrible experience. What did we learn? What will we do differently in the future?

We can practice how to bring out the best in ourselves and in others.

We can rewire our brains to more naturally respond in loving, kind, and compassionate ways. We can imagine "as if" until we become peaceful, kind, loving, compassionate and joyful.

Meditation is learning to penetrate each moment of living with the purifying flames of awareness.

Chapter 24

NO LONGER THE VICTIM

Meditation has the ability to transform the way we see ourselves and the world. A powerful outcome is the ability to let go of a victim mentality. How a person experiences life can be divided into three different categories:

1. **We think the outside world creates our experience.** Something happens in our external world, and we allow it to create certain thoughts, emotions, feelings, and sensations. It might seem that the external circumstance *causes* us to think or feel in a certain way, but the experience is actually created within us. It may *seem* like someone or something makes us angry or happy, but we are the ones choosing.

When we think we want new cars or relationships, what we really want is the feeling that those things will give us. We want to feel happy, loved, safe, or whatever the specific *experience* is that we desire, the one we might think we don't have, the one we might think can only be created by changing our external circumstances.

2. **We think that our internal processes create our experience.** We blame our thoughts and feelings for why we are experiencing life in a certain way. But thoughts are just electrical impulses, and feelings are just a mixture of various bio-chemicals. We sometimes assume we're irritated because of what is happening outside of us when, in fact, it's just the rising and falling away of a thought or a hormonal experience. Perhaps you can relate to feeling compelled to speak and act in unskillful ways that are driven by a thought, emotion or sensation. Some people assume that we have no control over our thoughts or feelings.

3. **We realize that we can choose our experience.** We have the power to create our experience of life regardless of our circumstances or thoughts or emotions. All it requires is for you to make the decision of how you want to experience life, then create and cultivate that experience going forward.

My dear friend Laura was diagnosed with cancer two years ago. It was devastating news and, I'm sure, carried much fear and anxiety. But I was so proud of the way she proactively decided how she wanted to go through the process. She decided early on that she wanted the experience to be transformational and wanted it to be an opportunity for her to cherish her friendships and her family. Whenever things got tough, whenever the pain and the treatments were excruciating, she would ask herself, **"How do I want to experience this situation?"** She didn't want to wallow in self-pity or ask, "Why me?" She looked for ways to respond with love and kindness to herself and to those around her. She wondered how she might inspire others by her actions. She is my role model for how we can experience the best and worst of life in a proactive and positive way.

Deciding to be happy has an incredible benefit. By focusing our energy on happiness, we create more energy to work with. We create more energy to change ourselves and the world for the better. Life doesn't have to seem so difficult.

You have this **incredible power within you** to decide how you want to experience life and where to put your energy—and meditation is the time-tested tool for rediscovering, tapping into, and cultivating this power within you. Start each day with deciding to be happy, and every other decision will become much easier to make.

Chapter 25

THE ULTIMATE FREEDOM

These practices are designed to help us find and experience unlimited freedom—a freedom beyond all others. It is the inner freedom that liberates us from the mercurial mental and emotional ups and downs of daily living.

When we were children, most of us thought of freedom as the ability to stay up late or watch TV, and we thought that was what happiness was all about. Then, as we became teenagers, we wanted the freedom to be with our friends, and we thought that would bring us happiness. Then we got out of the house and away from our parents and wanted the freedom that being on our own would bring, the freedom that money could buy, the freedom to do things we thought would make us happy. This desire for freedom in some form or fashion seems to be an important part of our psyches.

So here we are today. At whatever point you are in your life, you are here, right now. When you think about being free in this moment, what comes to mind? What is the freedom you desire?

It's powerful to acknowledge that even though we have grown up, we may still feel enslaved to our old ways of thinking about ourselves and the world. We might still be enslaved to this old idea of freedom.

In a superficial way, freedom is sometimes described as an ability to chase after any desire we have. "I want what I want, when I want it." We want the freedom to eat what we want to eat, to drink what we want to drink, the freedom to act on any whim that strikes us. But acting on any whim that arises is actually no freedom at all. In fact, it becomes the **worst** kind of imprisonment. We are imprisoned by our desires, forced to act on them, unable to withstand the feelings of withdrawal that arise if we do not keep chasing after every whim. It turns out that *not* acting on every whim or desire is the *first* step toward ultimate happiness. When we become willing to examine what these whims are all about, then we start to see the world and ourselves at a deeper level of richness, of fullness, of true reality, of true freedom.

You are the one you've been waiting for.

You are the only person who can transform your life.

We often put ourselves in the prison of limiting thoughts and actions. We keep seeking freedom from what is. Instead, we can learn to harness present awareness into a freedom to be *with* whatever is, a freedom with far less judgment and far move love and compassion, a freedom founded in curiosity and non-preference. The whole world begins to open up as possibilities. The desire for this ultimate freedom is one of the tools we can harness to find the long-lasting peace and happiness we've been looking for all along. As adults, we are no longer constrained by our parents or our past, but sometimes *we* allow ourselves to be. We may feel constrained by our old ways of thinking and our unskillful habits or constrained by our emotions, constrained by our illusions about what life is about, or constrained by what we think we are supposed to be doing. It's easy to get lost in the shackles of illusions that keep us from being completely happy and at peace. The *only* obstacle to more freedom and happiness is our own misguided way of thinking.

We can learn to focus our desire on the **inner freedom of choice**. Emotions or thoughts will continue to arise. We *always* have the freedom to choose *if* we react and then *how* to react.

In *Wake Up to Your Life*, Ken McLeod gives an eloquent description of how bringing attention to our thoughts, emotions and sensation can free us from their hold on us. He suggests the following process for dismantling old unskillful patterns.

1. **Recognize:** Whenever we have sensations or emotions or thoughts that cause a senses of struggle or suffering within us, we pay attention to them. Instead of avoiding them, we see them as opportunities for reflection.

2. **Dis-identify:** We can begin to see these sensations, emotions, or thoughts are *not* who we fundamentally are. *Thoughts only have power if we give it to them. Emotions only have power if we give it to them.* When we dis-identify with our thoughts and emotions and sensations, we are free to redirect our energy to more skillful responses.

3. **Develop a practice:** We practice not identifying with them again and again—it takes practice. Each time a thought or emotion or sensation arises, we have an opportunity to form a new habit, by being aware, reflecting upon it and dis-identifying with it, so that we can create a more skillful response/behavior. We continue practicing whenever they arise, until slowly their hold on us diminishes.

When concentration, awareness, and positive imagery become habits, then we are truly free to live our lives in peace, regardless of what arises.

But let's not wait for some magical day when we get it right every time. Let's start working at it now, with each thought and emotion a fresh opportunity to practice, and, with each opportunity, we open ourselves to this incredible freedom little by little. Over time, our lives do become magical in the sense of wonder and deep happiness that comes naturally from the experience of inner freedom. We have everything we need right now, in this moment, to experience the ultimate freedom of choosing to be happy, regardless of our external circumstances, regardless of our old thoughts and habits

You are the one you've been waiting for. Now is the moment to begin.

Why wait one moment longer?

Chapter 26

THE FINAL WORD

"When we are fully present in the moment, decisions arise as needed."

We can train ourselves to stay open, vulnerable, and curious about the experience of living, instead of focusing on what someone else says the answers are or must be. We can live life as an open question, instead of a definitive answer. **When we think we know the answer, we shut down to other possibilities.**

We can try out new ideas and still be open to the possibility of new information, new data, new perspectives, and approaches. How can we truly know in a constantly changing world? We can practice getting comfortable with uncertainty. What would that feel like? One way to explore the answer is to experiment with "not knowing." Here's a great practice by Gil Fronsdal, a well-known meditation teacher at Spirit Rock Retreat Center in California:

A simple but profound way to practice not knowing is to add "I don't know" to every thought. This is most effective in meditation when the mind has quieted down. So, for example, if the judgment arises, "This is a good meditation session" or "This is a bad meditation session," respond with, "I don't know." Follow any thought like "I can't manage this," "I need...,' or "I am..." with "I don't know." Like the bumper sticker that reads, "Question authority," the phrase "I don't know" questions the authority of everything we think.

Repeating the words "I don't know" allows us to question tightly held ideas. Done thoroughly, "I don't know" can pull the rug out from under our most cherished beliefs. All too often we don't question our beliefs. And, since virtually every train of thought has some implicit belief, when we question our thoughts, we question these beliefs.

Not knowing does not mean you don't know. It doesn't require us to forget everything we have known or to suspend all interpretations of a situation. **Not knowing means not being limited by what we know**, *holding what we know lightly so that we are ready for it to be*

*different. Maybe things are this way. But maybe they
are not.*

Meditation is the process of undoing, unlearning, and disentangling
from the past, and creating a whole new way of showing up in the
present without worrying so much about the future. I wish you the
very best on this amazing journey.

RECOMMENDED READING

If you would like to dive deeper into the various meditation topics we have discussed, the following books might be of use:

- *The Relaxation Response* by Dr. Herbert Benson

- *Awakening the Buddha Within* by Lama Surya Das

- *Wherever You Go There You Are* by Jon Kabat-Zinn

- *Happy Birthday to You!* by Dr. Seuss

- *Happiness: A Guide to Developing Life's Most Important Skill* by Matthieu Ricard

- *Flourish* by Martin Seligman

- *Turning the Mind into an Ally* by Sakyong Mipham

- *The Stories We Live By: Personal Myths and the Making of the Self* by Dan P. McAdams

- *Wake up to Your Life* by Ken McLeod

Janet Nima Taylor, MBA, has twenty years of experience as a corporate executive and trainer in the business world, and she is passionate about helping people change their behavior to create positive habits.

She has been practicing various forms of meditation since high school, and five years ago, she founded the daily meditation program Serenity Pause, which helps individuals incorporate more peace and calm into their lives.

She is also the director of the Temple Buddhist Center in Kansas City, Missouri as well as the executive director of the Dzoghchen Foundation, a national nonprofit organization with a focus on Buddhist practices and meditation.

In April 2013, in order to deepen her own daily practice, she took her monastic vows with her teacher of fifteen years, Lama Surya Das.

Made in the USA
Lexington, KY
24 February 2015